CW00498476

When the Spirit Moves You

A new life on a sub-tropical island

Geraldine Ann Ford

Published in 2014 revised 2022 by FeedARead.com
Publishing – Arts Council funded

I lived on La Gomera from October 2000 to June 2002. I
started writing this book a few years ago and there have been
a few changes on La Gomera. The hydrofoil now goes to Valle
Gran Rey, so you don't have to drive across the island. This
book is based on true events but some names and identifying
details have been changed to protect the privacy of
individuals. I have written with sensitivity at all times.

Email: geraldineannford@gmail.com - you can also find me
on Facebook and Instagram. Some of my poetry is on
YouTube and SoundCoud. I have included 24 of my poems
in this book.

This book is dedicated to my father, Leslie Gordon Ford, who
encouraged me to write from a young age. A special thank you
to my wonderful son and daughter, Joley, and Abby, for
putting up with my eccentricities over the years.

Chapter One

Swapped life in England
for life on a sun soaked island,
leaving behind satin wet pavements
and stair rods of rain.

Sun sets over this sub-tropical island,
in the Canary Archipelago -
an oasis in the desert.

Home is where I lay my head,
listening to the beat of a distant drum,
calling me to black sanded beaches
on this island of dreams.

Dreams are to be lived, not perpetually locked away, but dreams are often stowed away and for good reason. Children are for life, and I adore mine, but now they are in their twenties I feel it's time for me to embark on a journey of exploration and hopefully find a bit more of myself at the same time. It's an inherent feeling and one that will not go away until fully explored. I intend to make the year 2000 a memorable one.

Searching for a new milieu in a different part of the world would be frightening for some, but I'm looking forward to a new adventure on La Gomera; a sub-tropical island I have never seen before and only recently heard of. Not being able to speak Spanish will prove quite a challenge because there are very few English people on the island.

Saying goodbye to my sister-in-law, Eileen, at four thirty in the morning is emotional to say the least. She has kindly let me stay for the last three months and I will be eternally grateful for her generosity. She laughingly says with me going the house will be like the 'Marie

3

Celeste'. My family and I pile into the two cars parked on her driveway which are already filled with my luggage. Dreading the goodbyes at Gatwick I try to be cheerful, but I can sense the mounting tension.

It's not long before I'm at the airport moving nearer to the front of the queue to have my cases weighed. I push out positive energy to the attractive young lady handling the luggage, in the hope she'll be sympathetic. My sister's partner, Lyndon, does not look confident, and the closer we get the worse he looks as he eyes my two enormous suitcases. When it comes to my turn the expression on the steward's face is not promising but I continue to think positive thoughts.

"You are four times over the limit, and it will cost you two hundred and thirty pounds," she says with the look of utter amazement.

Lyndon looks like he's about to pass out. I knew the cases were heavy but eighty kilos over is a lot of excess; for a few seconds my positive energy seeps away. I explain to the stewardess that I had telephoned the airline the previous day to ask if I could take two cases onto the plane and they had said yes. She leaves to talk to her supervisor while I quickly count the sterling in my purse. Well, what else can I do? I'm not going anywhere without my luggage.

"Gel, there must be something you can take out. You can't pay that amount of money."

"I'm not going on holiday Lyndon I'm going to live out there and I need everything I've packed."

"But …"

"Don't worry it's going to be okay."

On returning the young lady looks solemn but she's letting me go through and with no charge. I think she just wants to be rid of my huge cases and me as the queue is now snaking further and further back; a few of my fellow travellers are beginning to look disgruntled.

"I don't believe it Gel, you're so lucky." Lyndon keeps repeating as we walk back to the rest of the family and I'm trying not to look too triumphant.

My family and I walk towards the departure lounge, and I start to feel peculiar around the solar plexus or is it that McDonalds breakfast we just ate. My son is telling me that gate forty-five is closing soon and we hug and kiss. This is it! My son and my daughter are trying hard not to show how upset they are and I'm trying to be strong for all of us.

Walking through the doors I fight back the tears. Don't turn round I tell myself, keep walking, but like most people I have to have another look. My kids and my dear sister Lynn are crying, and Lyndon looks as if he can't believe I'm actually doing it. I want to run and cuddle my babies, well they are still my babies, to tell them it's okay I won't go; instead, I turn away now choking on my tears as I have my passport checked. A light is flashing to remind me that gate forty-five will be closing soon, so I hurry on.

Mounting the steps of the plane I'm hardly aware of how I got there. I manage to find my seat and fasten the seat belt while taking great gulps of oxygen into my lungs and trying desperately to suppress my sobs. The euphoria I felt half an hour ago is waning and all I can see in my mind's eye is my son and daughter crying in each other's arms. "For goodness sake, cheer up!" I had said to them earlier. "It's not that far away and you're coming to see me soon." Now I feel like a complete heel, a selfish mother leaving her children to get on with their own lives. Well, isn't that what they're supposed to do at their age?

Refusing the artificial looking breakfast, the air hostess is trying to place in front of me, is not difficult, as I'm feeling sick with emotion. I can only manage to sip small amounts of water from a plastic bottle. Sitting next to me is a married couple who eat their way through breakfast and a tub of Pringles each; they then order a whisky and soda and a vodka and tonic. On holiday or not, I couldn't drink at 9.30 in the morning. And now the lady's extremely large arm (no offence) is taking up all the room on the armrest and the man in front of me is pushing his seat back almost crushing my knees in the process; my little bit of space is shrinking into oblivion.

Trying to read my paperback I realise I'm reading the same paragraph over and over again with a lump in my throat the size and texture of a tennis ball. My thoughts continually fly back to the airport, and I re-live the scene several times before I see part of The Canary Islands framed in the aircraft window. Mountains rise up ceremoniously, the sun is shining and it's a beautiful clear day. I'm winging my way to my new life on La Gomera, leaving behind the upsurge in political correctness, the rain soaked streets and the ever increasing price of petrol. Soon I will be happily ensconced in a small apartment I have never seen before, on the side of a mountain on La Gomera, an island I have never previously visited. A few people, not my true friends of course, who already think I'm loopy now think I am totally deranged.

Feeling less maudlin at Tenerife Airport is a good thing as I need get a taxi to Los Christianos. Waiting forty-five minutes is bad enough but people are starting to push in the queue; I am not amused. Pulling a taxi door open and throwing my rucksack onto the back seat before anyone else does ensures me a ride. Five minutes later I'm regretting my impetuosity. I'm beginning to think this maniacal taxi driver is trying to kill me off before I reach my destination. Only a short time has passed, and we've reached the port already. The driver has stopped so suddenly that my nose ends up precariously six inches away from the windscreen. Glad to be out of the taxi I give him extra pesetas in the hope he will help me, but it does not seem to be working. He leaves me standing mouth agape with my gargantuan suitcases left on the pavement outside the ticket office, while he dashes off to collect another fare from the airport; a potential heart attack if ever I saw one.

A sweet young Spanish lady in the ticket office, who speaks a little English, takes pity on me, and offers to find assistance; I sigh with relief. Suffering from the painful condition of cervical spondylosis means I can't lift the cases on my own. A 'drop dead' gorgeous young man dressed in blue, obviously a steward, is coming towards me with a huge grin on his handsome face and he grabs the handles of both cases. He utters some Spanish expletive when he feels the weight and I'm sure he thinks I have a couple of dead bodies in them as he eyes me suspiciously. Swinging them expertly up into the container he says, in the most gorgeous accent.

"You stay for a year?"

"Yes, maybe longer. Who knows?" I laugh cheekily as I walk away towards the café. What a hunk! I have to remind myself I'm not going to la Gomera to flirt with young Spanish men, but to write.

Slightly happier now, I decide to buy a big sticky doughnut and a cappuccino. I'm in need of a little comfort so my healthy eating will have to start tomorrow. From my table there is a good view of the port of Los Christianos, and I start to take in the scenery around me.

Little white houses with red tiled roofs sit on the sunny slopes stretching down to the harbour, where there are boats and yachts of all shapes and sizes rocking gracefully on the water.

Feeling the need to stretch my legs I walk over to the town where many ex-pats live. A quick walk around Los Christianos is more than enough. Women with numerous gold chains hanging round their necks are making my neck feel sore. Overweight, bare-chested middle aged men, some with the cracks of their bums showing above the waistbands of their shorts, are making me feel somewhat overdressed. Swiftly I walk back to the port. I'm sure there is a more salubrious part of Los Christianos but I'm not going to hang around to find out.

People are boarding the boat, so I'd better get moving. A little later I'm climbing the steps to the second deck which means I have a beautiful view of Tenerife. Immersed in sunlight I marvel at it sparkling on the waves like a million tiny shards of glass. Turning to see Mount Teide in the distance with a band of white cottony cloud just below the snow-capped peak fills me with awe. The turquoise ocean beneath me looks inviting and I'm content to stand at the railings gazing at the sea, in which I've had a lifelong affinity. Memories of my childhood came back to me. I remembered how ecstatic I felt when we arrived at a seaside town, and I spied that wonderful blue sea in the distance; although in England it can sometimes be grey but it's still beautiful.

Engines begin to purr and burst into life as we slowly edge away from the harbour wall, taking me closer to my new home. Climbing more steps, I have an even better view of Tenerife and Mount Teide, unfortunately I have to look past three middle-aged men and one of them obviously thinks I'm looking at him. "I was looking at the mountain behind you not the one in front hanging over your trousers," I mumble to myself and quickly move to the other side of the boat. We enter deeper water and I feel at one with the ocean. The sea around the boat now looks purple as we steam ahead, leaving a trail of white foam.

A short distance behind us the Fred Olsen Express comes into sight and as I watch it getting closer, I can clearly see the name on the side, 'Benchijigua' (pronounced b-e-n-c-h-i-i-i-u-a); I'm supposed to be on that boat. At the port I realised I had bought the wrong tickets but even I did not have the nerve to ask anyone, not even the hunky young steward, to move my hefty luggage to another container. The Express overtakes us and reaches San Sebastian about twenty minutes before we arrive. I hope my new landlord, who is meeting me, does not think I've changed my mind.

We arrive after an hour and a half and having thoroughly enjoyed the boat trip I'm rather pleased I boarded the wrong one. We slide up closer to the harbour wall and I can see down below a brown truck with GEL written on the windscreen. Waving frantically and pointing to myself Pedro soon realises who I am and waves back. He is shouting something, but his words are lost on the wind. My new landlord doesn't know what I look like unless my friend, who already lives in Valle Gran Rey, has described me to him; attractive but rather bohemian, pleasantly plump, short hair and acts like forty-eight going on twenty-five.

Beginning to feel tired I look at my watch, three thirty and I've been up since four o'clock this morning but seeing their friendly faces as I walk down the steps of the boat, soon cheers me up. Pedro and his girlfriend Lucy are all smiles, and they kiss me on both cheeks; my friend's six-year old daughter launches herself at me. Pedro gasps as he swings my cases into the boot of his truck; I smile apologetically, and he laughs. What friendly people. I'm sure I'm going to like it here.

We have to travel to the other side of the island and as we climb higher, I feel I'm on some sort of fairground ride and start to feel sick. I'm beginning to regret having eaten that sugary doughnut; although I'm sure my feeling queasy is a combination of food intolerances, lack of sleep, spent emotion, the long journey and Pedro's twenty-one year old truck with little suspension. Not that I'm complaining of course.

"Geraldine, look!" Lucy says as she points to the view.

What a magnificent sight! Mount Teide looking serene and the cerulean ocean spreading behind us; for a few minutes I forget how awful I feel as I look all around me and admire my new environment. My ears pop as we climb higher, then to my relief we start to descend. We are nearly there, I mistakenly think, until I see a sign which says 20 kilometres to Valle Gran Rey. We drive up the winding roads again and as we get higher there is more greenery; the cool wind is certainly a welcome relief. Lucy says I look good after such a long journey. I don't feel good, but I smile and make the effort.

"We are coming into the valley soon," Pedro calls with obvious delight. Sitting up straight with anticipation I forget my tiredness. Will it look like the pictures I have seen, or will I be disappointed I wonder?

"Look at your new home Geraldine," he sings my name as we round a bend and Valle Gran Rey (Valley of the great King) comes into sight. As we enter this huge canyon, with two six hundred foot cliffs on either side, the sinuous road plunges and the picturesque villages look minute. Sweeping down the verdant mountainside

10

in front of us is a spectacular view and at the bottom the Atlantic Ocean glimmering in the sun.

On our left Pedro points out a restaurant school where they train chefs which is integrated into the cliff. The architecture is by the famous artist Cesar Manrique and the view from the restaurant terrace is magnificent. We then continue down the meandering road towards my new apartment.

"Oh, it's beautiful Pedro," I hear myself say and then I lapse into silence. The pictures I saw in England undoubtedly did it justice and I am certainly not disappointed; it feels and looks wonderful.

"This place is very holy," he says with conviction.

Holy, spiritual, whatever you choose to call it the energy is tangible, and I feel I have come home. A few more bends and we arrive at Casa de Pedro a block of eight apartments built into the mountainside.

Feeling slightly bemused I look at my new habitat as my friend Annabelle comes out to greet me. There are so many steps and how we manage to heave my two cases into my flat I do not know. I wonder how on earth they move furniture in or out but at least I will end up slim living here. From all the windows of my new apartment and terrace the view is stunning. I drink in the beauty of nature all around me, knowing I've made the right decision.

Walking down a flight of steps and then up another, left past Pedro and Lucy's flat then up wooden steps to Annabelle's flat, it's not surprising I arrive breathless; now I know I'm living on the side of a mountain. Doing this trek a few times before nightfall because I need the company, is tiring, especially after such a long journey. I unpack most of my things but decide to leave the rest until the morning. Sheer exhaustion is about to overcome any feelings of excitement. I take a shower with the intention of going to bed.

It was difficult to sleep last night after I found a huge round cockroach sitting on top of the bathroom door with his antennae swaying menacingly back and forth. I nearly took the next plane back to England but instead I decided to barricade it in with towels, so it couldn't attack me during the night. Annabelle tried to convince me this morning that cucarachas (cockroaches) are not usually found in new apartments, but she reminded me that it has been empty for a while. I decide to buy some poison just the same which is unusual for me as normally I don't like to kill anything, but cockroaches send a shiver down my spine.

Pedro loves nature and insects, but he doesn't like cucarachas either, so I don't feel such a wimp now. Cucarachas … cucarachas, do you remember that catchy song some crazy people made about cockroaches? Well, I couldn't get it out of my head last night, no wonder I didn't sleep much. Why does anyone in their right mind want to sing about cockroaches anyway?

Sitting on the terrace I look at the amazing views with all thoughts of large insects pushed to the back of my mind as I take in the panoramic picture before me. Waiting for the sun to come up I look at my watch, it's nearly ten o'clock. Dawn breaks at seven thirty but I think the cockerel down below is a bit out of sync, as he was crowing at three thirty this morning. The sun does not rise high enough above the mountain until much later. Now it's just peeping over the top bathing everything in brilliant light, like liquid gold slowly pouring down to the bottom of the valley. A writers' and artists' paradise!

Below my terrace there is a footpath and I see the locals working their land. One of the women walking past is balancing an enormous basket of lettuces on her head and I gaze at her with admiration, wondering how on earth the basket stays put. I shout, "Hola" and "buenos dias," the only Spanish words I know, and they shout back and wave.

There are a few goats tied up in front of the apartments, a storing shed made of stone is a few feet from the path under the terrace; a few yards in front of that there's a dilapidated little stone building for the chickens. I'm sure the chickens don't mind the state of their abode as long as they are fed. Early this morning I heard the cock crowing and later the goats were bleating; followed by an almighty racket I did not recognise at first. Well, there's not much call for donkeys in Kent is there.

Sitting here looking at the sights is intoxicating even without a gin and tonic. To my left is a large white bungalow surrounded by papaya trees as tall as pike staffs and farmed terraces are all around us. The land has to be terraced because of the terrain which I wouldn't like to work on. In front of my apartment are banana trees, the thick succulent leaves rustling in the breeze, and on the next terrace an abundance of vegetables are growing and more banana trees. Earthy smells emanate from the thick flora and the fertile ground around me; the sweet scent of citrus fruit from the many orange and lemon trees wafts under my nose, teasing my taste buds. Date palms are growing everywhere, and I can even see a few high up on the mountain ledges and further down the valley there is a huge clump.

La Gomera is known for its palm trees and about one hundred thousand grow here. Palm syrup is extracted from these trees and is deliciously sinful, but not especially good for one's figure. The trees are attractive with a splash of orange sprouting from the middle of the palm fronds where the dates grow. Beyond this delightful valley is a wedge of glorious blue ocean.

Yesterday I was in England with satin wet pavements caused by stair rods of rain; today I'm in La Gomera. This sun-drenched island, where they do not have much rain, is now my home and I pinch myself to see if I'm awake. One day I'm living in Kent and the next I'm living in exotic Valle Gran Rey. I feel rather strange to say the least and I'm sure I will do for a few weeks before I regain my equilibrium. Some people think I'm already strange to uproot myself in the first place; my answer to them is, "Everyone else is mad, I'm normal." Actually, I don't really want to be normal, whatever normal is … it sounds boring.

Chapter Two

Green valley stretches
to the cerulean sea
glinting like crystal.

La Playa (the beach)

Today I'm going on a walkabout, and I set off early in the day with my rucksack and a large bottle of water; I don't want to be caught out by the siesta. It takes forty minutes to reach La Playa from my apartment. Impressed with the black-sanded beaches and the rugged coastline I stop to inhale the fresh brackish air and can taste the salt on my tongue.

I continue walking into town towards the harbour where I find the mobile phone shop. Do I really want a mobile phone in this heavenly place? Will its continuous bleep invade my newfound liberty? Well, I definitely need one so I can stay in contact with my kids. But trying to make the young assistant understand I want to buy a pay-as-you-go mobile telephone proves to be rather difficult and I come away disappointed. I'll have to come back with Annabelle as her Spanish is good and mine is almost non-existent. Must make a mental note to start learning Spanish as soon as possible, otherwise I'm not going to be able to communicate with the locals.

The Ferreteria is next, what we call the ironmongers. Unable to find the larger shop, which Annabelle told me to go to, I settle for a smaller one which doesn't look too promising. Not noticing the counter flap is pulled back I walk straight through so I can see things on the shelves, immediately being ushered out by a not too friendly gentleman in his middle years who appears out of nowhere. Thankfully he disappears back into his hidey hole and leaves me in the hands of a young lad who doesn't seem to notice my red face.

The next twenty minutes is like something from a comedy programme. I want hooks so I hook my finger and point to some locked behind the glass; anyone would think they were the crown jewels. Light bulbs you would believe easy to mime but whether the young lad is none too bright or my miming is not as good as it used to be, I'm not sure. Charades used to be my favourite game at Christmas, and I was rather good at it, even if I do say so myself. Sticking my arm up in the air and turning my hand as if to screw a light bulb worked in the end, as a light has switched on in his head; great, now we're getting somewhere. Surveying the shelves, I point to a few other things I need, which includes a wash basket right at the top and he duly collects all my purchases and puts them on the counter. Coat hangers next, this will be fun. Hanging my arms out to the side and making myself look like a coat hanger is not proving successful, ingenious though I thought it was, the young lad in the shop has no idea what I want. Reaching into my rucksack I grab a small pad and pen and draw, to the best of my ability, a coat hanger; he rushes out to the back of the shop and produces a dozen wooden coat hangers. Eureka! I say "mucho gracias" to the young lad who has been extremely patient.

While putting my goods in the wash basket, so I can carry it under my arm, I suddenly feel quite drained. But I'm also pleased that I managed, after a bit of hard work, to buy the things I needed. The sun is high in the sky and it's getting hotter, but I'm fascinated by my new surroundings. I marvel at the amount of space there is to park a car, if you want to visit the shops or go to the beach, not a multi-storey in sight; indeed, if there was one it would be incongruous to say the least. When I stop for a late lunch carrying my wash basket full of an assortment of household items, I certainly don't look like a tourist. Most tourists here are walkers carrying half a bungalow on their backs, wearing khaki hats, some even with corks swinging from the brim, and holding metal pronged sticks; I presume they are to poke somebody with if they lag behind.

Feeling hot and tired after walking for so long I telephone for a taxi, extravagant I know, but I do not feel like walking up the steep valley road. Making the taxi driver understand where I want to go is fairly easy. He grins at me and looks amused as I struggle clumsily into the cab with my goods, just managing to close the door behind me. Sitting back against the seat I admire the scenery from a different perspective, noticing things I hadn't seen on the way down. What a stunning valley this is!

Climbing the steps to my apartment a short while later I realise it's early evening already. There's still some sunlight shining behind the mountain turning the fluffy clouds a pretty pink and making them look like candyfloss. It reminds me of long lazy days by the sea with my parents and siblings; I want to reach up and take one.

Eager for a swim the next day I don my swimming costume, which I think looks rather attractive. Annabelle meets me on the beach after dropping her daughter off at school and I can't help noticing her bikini as much as I try not to stare. It consists of three tiny triangles elegantly tied to her cellulite free body and yes, I'm envious. Annabelle looks like she's just stepped off the catwalk and I look like two people trying to get out of a sack; my spirit flags but not for long. Soon I feel as free as the seagulls bobbing up and down on the oscillating waves. Floating on my back with arms outstretched I let the sun warm through every muscle in my body, especially my neck. Feeling at one with the Atlantic Ocean and putting things into perspective I realise I am a minuscule dot in the universe; yes, even I can be a minute speck floating on this vast expanse of water.

More exercise is needed, so I swim out to a large flat rock and sit for a while. I notice the promenade to the left lined with squatty palms and just below this many small slippery rocks and rock pools; a haven for wildlife and for children searching for anything that moves, while parents watch on. The rock I'm sitting on is slimy and it feels like wet moss as I bathe in the sun. I have such an affinity with the ocean; maybe I was a mermaid in a past life I laugh to myself. Deep blue sky is mirrored in the water about me as I slither back into the sea and swim to shore. This place is a panacea and I feel healthy and at peace with myself.

Managing to get a bus back to Casa de la Seda saves me the forty-minute climb, but I promise myself I will undertake this walk soon. There is a cool breeze, and the sun is going down behind the mountain reflecting onto a few lint clouds, turning them pale orange.

Walking along the path from the main road I meet some of the locals sitting outside their pretty houses clad with purple and pink bougainvillea prolific in this part of the world. I can't help staring at a colossal poinsettia on the other side of the path; it makes the puny ones we buy in Marks and Spencer at Christmas look tiny in comparison. My neighbours greet me happily and I answer them in my stilted attempt at Spanish. Receiving a few funny looks when practising this unfamiliar language means I must be doing something wrong; no doubt it's my Southeast London accent. I must make enquiries at the 'Escuela de Idiomas', the Language School, which is in La Calera, a village further down the Valley. Apparently, the head teacher came from mainland Spain, and it took her a long time to get used to Gomera Spanish, as it's different to Castilian Spanish. Personally, I don't care what Spanish it is as long as I can communicate without having to play charades every time I want to be understood.

Water is scarce and treasured on La Gomera. A greater part of it comes from fountains and bed currents and the lack of rain affects agriculture and humans alike. There are tanks, wells, dams, and reservoirs all over the island. Nearing the steps to my flat I can hear the welcome sound of rushing water. The farmers have enormous water taps in various places and one is just under my terrace pouring water into the irrigation channel below, where it is much needed. Listening to the sound of running water is bliss, as I sit on the terrace a few minutes later drinking my coffee. I have always wanted a water feature in my garden, now I have one, and I didn't have to pay for it.

The following day I stay at home to catch up with some writing and reading. My new book, which I bought yesterday, is all about the Canary Islands and I am eager to get started. Sitting looking at the vista for a while, I thank my lucky stars that I'm here at all. Actually, I have to thank Annabelle, because it was after speaking to her on the telephone in England that I decided to come to La Gomera. I had already made up my mind I wanted sun, sea, mountains and peace and she told me besides these things there were also beautiful green valleys and a rainforest.

"Right," I said, "that's where I'm going to live."

"What do you mean? You haven't even seen it yet?"

"I can see it in my mind's eye, and I can feel it, so I'll start packing up as soon as I've told the kids."

"Geraldine, I'm amazed!"

"Well, I know I'm going to live abroad somewhere hot and La Gomera sounds perfect" or words to that effect. Four months later I was ready with my two large suitcases, which were in danger of bursting open.

The Canary Islands are situated about seventy miles from Africa. It is said that along with the Azores and Cape Verde they could be the highest peaks of the fabled Atlantis, which legend says disappeared after its cataclysmic destruction; I like this idea, it sounds romantic.

La Gomera is one of seven major islands within the Canary Archipelago and is almost circular in shape and only 372 Sq. km, sometimes referred to as a floating wheel in the middle of the Atlantic Ocean. Most people have only heard of the four larger islands Tenerife, Fuerteventura, Gran Canaria and Lanzarote; the three smaller islands La Palma, La Gomera, and El Hierro are not so well known. The two latter islands are the smallest and El Hierro hardly has any tourists. It is said to be like paradise, especially if you see the stunning scenery by walking round the island; the people are friendly and hospitable. When I told my friends and family, I was going to live on La Gomera they looked at me with blank expressions on their faces.

A great part of La Gomera's seashores have high cliffs and the island is volcanic as you can tell from the colour of the sand. Recently in England I watched an interesting television programme about La Palma. It still has a live volcano and apparently, it's likely to erupt within the next one hundred years and half the island could slide into the ocean causing a tsunami. There's the likelihood of it flooding parts of America and the backlash could go as far as England's South coast. Not the sort of programme one should watch when planning to start a new life on these islands.

Later in the afternoon I go to the beach with Annabelle and her daughter, Lilly. We only stay for a couple of hours because the last bus from La Playa is at 6.30 in the evening. I decide to ignore this fact and do some late shopping. Annabelle and Lilly return home on the scooter and I go for a stroll, then to the supermacado (supermarket). Walking up and down the aisles trying to find what I want takes ages and a sweet young assistant helps me as much as she can. Having found most of the things I need I give up searching frantically for Branston pickle and English mustard, wondering how I will live without them. I tap out the only local taxi number on my mobile but there is no answer. One of the assistants takes the phone and tries again for me, to no avail. She shrugs apologetically and says they must have finished for the evening and hands me back the phone.

Incredulous, I look at my watch, which says it's only nine o'clock and I'm stranded with Lilly's body board and four bags of shopping; I will not endeavour to walk home with so much to carry and only a pair of flimsy sandals on. I'm beginning to worry so the only thing I can do is ring Annabelle and see if she can come down and fetch me on the scooter. Rummaging through my bag I realise I have left my diary indoors with Annabelle's phone number in it. By this time the shopkeeper is starting to lock up. My newly acquired friend Angela, you don't pronounce the g, kindly lets me stay with my bags and body board leaving trails of sand on the floor behind me. The only thing I can do is telephone Peter in England and ask him for Annabelle's number, providing he is home of course; I sigh with relief when he answers the phone.

"Peter, I'm so glad you're in."

"Gel, what's wrong?" He asks as I only spoke to him on the phone yesterday.

"Well, it's like this, I'm stuck down at the beach with four bags of shopping and Lilly's body board, the last bus left at 6.30 and I've just found out the taxis finish at 9 o'clock. I need to ring Annabelle so she can pick me up on the scooter and I've left her telephone number in the apartment," I told him without taking a breath. He laughs down the phone.

"Don't laugh, it's not funny, I'm stranded!"

"Well, what can I do?"

"Give me Annabelle's number."

"Oh right." I knew he was reaching for his little red book, and he read the number out to me.

"Thanks Peter, I'll speak to you soon. Don't want to use all my credit."

Soon after phoning Annabelle she arrives and apologises for not telling me about the taxis. She laughs about me ringing Peter in England for her number. We manage to fit the shopping and ourselves and the body board onto the scooter. What a relief! Waving to Angela we begin our slow ride back to Casa de la Seda; slow, because it's bad enough having the shopping on the scooter let alone me as well. Annabelle looks rather pensive to say the least and I say a silent prayer that we make it. Why is it that I go shopping and end up creating havoc in the process?

Making excuses again the following day for not walking home does not make me feel guilty, it's because I can't wear my trainers at the moment. When I first arrived, I walked down the valley road with what I thought were a very comfortable pair of soft leather pink sandals and ended up with great big blisters. I couldn't resist buying them in England, pink with embroidery and little mirrors, you know the sort of thing we used to wear in the early seventies; they go well with my favourite embroidered waistcoat with the gold tassels. My daughter says I'm going back to my hippie days and maybe I am; I felt like a free spirit then.

In a relatively short time, I feel at home in Valle Gran Rey, despite the fact that I cannot speak Spanish or German. I was surprised to hear so many German voices when I first arrived. The German population obviously discovered La Gomera a long time ago and many of them live here. They are not known for being over friendly, but most of them are polite and I soon get to know the sociable ones who speak excellent English.

I innocently remark to a Gomera bar owner, who is one of the few who speaks English, that there are not many Brits on La Gomera.

"We don't want any," he says; oblivious to the fact that I'm English and a customer spending money in his bar.

"Oh … and why is that?" I ask him feeling a little put out by his attitude.

"We don't want empty lager cans all over the beach and fighting in the bars," he retorts and goes off to serve another customer.

It's a shame he thinks most of us act in this way; maybe he went to an English football match in the nineteen eighties? Undesirable tourists, whether English, German or Spanish would not come to La Gomera anyway, because there are not enough night clubs and no fast food restaurants to keep them happy. I brush his remarks aside as I listen to him ranting on about this and that. He seems to have a chip on his shoulder the size of a house and it's uncanny how he looks and sounds like my ex-husband.

My German Friends

Going to the beach on my own does not bother me as I love my own company and at least I don't have to sit next to my sylph like friend in her minuscule bikini today.

Actually, everyone says I'm losing weight and looking extremely healthy with my newly acquired tan.

Sixteen years ago, I was introduced to, 'You Can Heal Your Life,' a best-selling book by Louise Hay. I was told to love myself fat or thin, but I wasn't quite ready for this revelation at the time, and I could not suppress my giggles. The mere sight of my gargantuan body, I was a size 20, with rolls of excess fat made me grimace into the mirror. I could have been paid good money advertising for 'Michelin' or 'Pirelli' and I found it extremely hard to learn to love myself; in retrospect, it was probably one of the best pieces of advice I have ever been given. However, I'm not saying all large people are lacking in self-esteem and I'm not suggesting that all overweight people suffer from comfort eating. Some people just love food, but there's no doubt about it though, I used to fall into all three categories.

I have always had an interest in Philosophy and religion but not organised religion. At quite a young age I came to realise that a religious person is not necessarily a spiritual being, although many are; sometimes they are judgemental and lack tolerance. We had a family next door to us when we were young and while the man was pleasant enough his wife, a religious fanatic, was always moaning. She seemed to dislike children and when my brother, Graham, sent a ball over their fence she complained bitterly about it. They had their church friends round on Sunday evenings, and they would sing hymns and bang the piano loudly. The music got louder and louder and my father would turn the television up; it was so funny. We would have Sunday Night at The London Palladium on full blast, and they'd be singing, 'Rock of Ages' at the top of their voices.

All this reminiscing is making me hungry. There are strong winds today and sand is blowing in my face, so I think it's time to leave. An umbrella just came somersaulting across the beach and nearly speared a topless bather; could have been a nasty case of cause and effect.

We do have extremely strong winds here, which can die down after a few minutes; some of them are what we call 'Caleema', and they come across from the Sahara. These winds are hot and are like standing in front of a fan heater bringing fine layers of sand, which can cause chest problems. Fortunately, it's not so much of a problem on La Gomera as it is on some of the other Canary Islands.

My plastic dryer on the terrace has to be held down with a lump of concrete because of the high winds. The last thing I want is my washing taking off down the valley, my knickers could end up in a banana plantation and my bras could be hanging in next door's Papaya trees; still, they could use them as hammocks. I smile to myself as I pack up my things and make my way to one of the many restaurants.

This succulent steak is delicious and I'm sorry if some of my readers are vegetarian. I tried to be a vegetarian once and it lasted about four months, until the wonderful aroma of sizzling bacon came wafting under my twitching nostrils; I'm afraid I switched back to being a carnivore.

I must say this gin and tonic being placed in front of me is large compared to the small measures they give you in England and it tastes so strong; I'm glad I'm not driving. My drink lasts me the whole of the meal and all of it so cheap. I hardly ever dined out in England unless I was being treated or wined and dined by the opposite sex. Actually, I'm off men at the moment, well I have been since June. Yes, I know it's only October but it's definite this time.

I suffered from mental abuse for many years when I was married and of course the children endured it too; you lose all respect for yourself, and your dreams begin to fade into nothingness. In the early 1980's I was given a book called, 'The Power of Positive Thought' and it changed my life. Finding my voice once more enabled me to become strong enough to divorce my husband, for reasons too numerous to mention. I began striving for new goals, the most important one being the need to keep a roof over the children's heads. I vowed to myself I would not talk about their father in a derogatory manner in front of them and I never did. A few years ago, they told me how much they admired and respected me for this. They said every time they went to their dad's for the weekend, he would say horrible things about me; it was obvious at the time because they would come home from his house sullen, confused, and distant. It is so unfair to the children when one or both of the estranged parents do this. How can you love your children and treat them in such an abominable way? It's tantamount to child abuse!

My goodness I am becoming heavy, it must be the gin. The waiter who is bringing me the bill is gorgeous, well there's no harm in looking is there. He's probably married with eight kids, a heavy drinker, a gambler, or even a serial killer, knowing my luck.

Chapter Three

Freedom's flame flickered,
captured with capriciousness
manacled mind
from work weary days.
Life lubricated, lucid;
suffused with sunshine, spent
in liberalised literary hours
on sun-soaked shores;
waves wash,
cleanse carefree days,
precious present pellucid,
seeping away like sieved sand.
Words written, worked,
creatively crafted,
poetical pieces, prose pouring,
from freedom's fire.

Fortunately, where I live in Valle Gran Rey there are a couple of English people, but most of the neighbours are Gomeras, so I have plenty of folk to practise my Spanish on. Annabelle told me yesterday the house next to our flats belongs to an English lady called Brenda and she's been living here for about thirteen years. Today I saw a lady walking under the terrace. She looked English, so I said hello and introduced myself and it was good to hear an English voice. Until I learn Spanish and maybe a little German it is going to be difficult to communicate.

The lady living in the next-door apartment is French. Paulette has been living here for eight years and speaks fluent Spanish. She wanted to start a new life and she also came to La Gomera after speaking on the phone to a friend. Paulette was exhausted after working for many years for the women's rights movement in France. We manage to communicate quite well, as she speaks some English and I speak a little French.

28

Pedro is often around, especially if we need help. He is kind and sometimes funny, although highly-strung as well. Many times, I hear him shout from his terrace upstairs, "Hola Geraldine," and he throws down mangoes, bananas and sometimes a big bag of oranges. He sends my post down in a carrier bag hanging on a piece of string; a friendly delivery service. I'm certainly eating more fruit and vegetables since I've been here, twice last week one of the farmers gave me mangoes and a large marrow and they are all so kind, despite thinking I'm a crazy English woman.

Waiting for the last bus I sit outside Las Jornadas, known as Bar Maria, which is a local landmark and one of the first restaurants built at La Playa. Besides being a lovely lady, Maria is also a good cook. Often when walking past Bar Maria I pop my head in and say good morning and invariably she's making something calorific, like doughnuts, and she insists on me having at least one piping hot dough ball; naughty but oh so delicious.

At first, I did not notice a middle aged couple also waiting for the bus, but I can hear their English voices as we form a short queue expecting the bus driver to open the doors at any moment. Climbing aboard we soon realise we're all going to Casa de la Seda and we start to chat. Bernie and Ann are staying with Brenda, my neighbour, and we instantly like one another; we all laugh when we find out we lived fifteen miles from each other in England.

The following evening Brenda kindly invites me into her house for dinner with her daughter Pia, Bernie and Ann and they make me feel very welcome. People say I'm brave for packing up and coming out to La Gomera to start a new life without having been here before but compared to what Brenda did fourteen years ago I do not feel courageous. She started a new life out here with two very young daughters, eventually building her own house with the help of friends. Trying to learn the language, work and feed the children at the same time must have been a challenge, to say the least. Her house is built into the side of the mountain, made from stone, and has an attractive little garden. Looking round I notice a pretty lampshade and I ask Brenda what it's made of, "a camel's scrotum", she replies.

Her daughters are beautiful girls brought up in a wonderful environment and they have a lovely freshness about them. Sadly, my own two have had to become 'streetwise', similar to young people in many countries across the globe. Like most mothers I still worry when they go to nightclubs, especially with so many drugs on the market. My son and daughter laugh at me for not being 'streetwise' and sometimes get annoyed because they think I put myself in danger.

I remember a day when Joe and Abby had been arguing for hours and I was so fed up I walked out with a poetry book and a note pad under my arm. I went for a long walk down by the river, which was ten or fifteen minutes from my house. Not wanting to be too near the families taking picnics and children trying to catch tadpoles in their fishing nets, I walked to a more secluded part of the meadows. Watching the swans and ducks on the river was a joy and I sat against a beautiful weeping willow tree, with its thick green branches; it kindly shaded me from the sun, and it felt like it was enfolding my being. I slowly began to relax and unwind and had a little meditation. It was a wonderful three hours away from it all, but when I returned home refreshed my eighteen year old daughter was not happy.

30

"Where have you been mother?" She asked as I walked through the front door. I knew as soon as I heard "mother" I was in for a telling off.

"What do you mean?" I answered trying to ignore her tone.

"You've been gone for hours. I didn't know where you were and you didn't take your mobile phone," she said with attitude.

"Maybe I wanted to leave my mobile behind, with you two arguing all morning I needed to get out of the house. I walked through the meadows and sat by the river, and it was absolute heaven." I knew this would cause a stir, but I didn't care. My newly found tranquillity was in ruins.

"Mum, do you realise you could have been attacked? There are some nasty characters on the estate nearby."

"Oh, for goodness sake, it comes to something when I can't even go for a quiet walk or hug a tree or two without having to report to my teenage daughter." Abby rolled her eyes in exasperation. I laugh at these memories.

The following afternoon I set out for La Playa to have a swim, but when I arrive, I'm not sure whether to leave my things on the beach or not. Annabelle assures me there is nothing to concern myself about and that my things will be quite safe. Swimming in the sea once again is bliss, but I keep looking over to see if my belongings are still where I left them. Just before I left England, I had a brand new mobile phone stolen and some money and straight-away the children accused me of not being diligent enough. "So, I'm idealistic, but why should I change because it can sometimes be a horrible world?" They admitted defeat, shook their heads, shrugged their shoulders, and sighed.

Feeling tired of this way of life I was eager to fly to my island in the sun; I'm not saying there is no crime on La Gomera but there is very little.

Walking back after my swim I can see Bernie and Ann on the beach, and they call to me, so I move to where they are sitting. My mobile begins to ring, an unwanted distraction. I take it out with me all the time as I like to hear from family and friends in England. True companions are so important, and I have some wonderful friends. Recently I've written to every one of them. I ended up with a severe case of writer's cramp and I do not want to see another postcard of Valle Gran Rey for a very long time. Unfortunately, the phone call is from my mum to tell me my daughter might have glandular fever and it's only two weeks since I arrived in Valle Gran Rey. Obviously, I'm upset, I am a mother, and my daughter has a history of illness, so I start to worry. Ann and Bernie take me to the nearest bar and buy me sangria, followed by a large creamy banana split and it cheers me up for a short while.

Brenda arrives to look at the sunset and I must admit it is beautiful. There are many couples on the beach and people sitting all along the promenade wall with their legs dangling over the side. The atmosphere is exciting and it's at times like these when you realise material things are not so important, but simple things in life like these amazing sunsets are essential to our very existence. There are many people impervious to mother-nature because they are so caught up in the material world, they forget to live.

Fingers of pink cloud stretch out from the horizon and the sun begins to drop in the sky. The nearer the sun gets to the ocean the quicker its descent and all of a sudden in a mass of golden light, it disappears. People begin to disperse, and Brenda comes into the bar to join us for a drink. Having lived here for a long time she knows most of the locals and the best restaurants and bars and we are not disappointed with her choice twenty minutes later.

Lola's is a good Spanish restaurant and when you see the locals coming in you know the food must be good. While we're waiting for our meals to arrive the men around the bar start to sing. It's a public holiday and soon they produce chakaras, four times the size of maracas, guitars and bandelas, which are like tiny banjos, and they all join in. When things happen spontaneously it's always more enjoyable and soon the four of us are tapping our feet and clapping to the music.

Having a sudden pang of conscience because I'm sitting here enjoying myself, while my daughter is languishing in England with possible glandular fever, I excuse myself and I take my phone outside. It's too noisy inside to speak to Abby, who answers straight-away. Suddenly it starts to rain really hard, and everyone comes out of the restaurant to look at the unexpected downpour. They've not had much rain for three years so it's a bit of a novelty. Abby laughs when I tell her what all the excitement is about. Sadly, England at the moment is suffering from torrential rain and floods across most of the country.

Returning to our table I leave the phone on the side because I'm expecting a telephone call from my friend Peter in Brighton. Tomorrow he's coming to La Gomera to share the apartment with me, but that's all he's going to be sharing despite what some people might think; we have been good friends for about thirteen years. For the last few weeks, I've been telling him about the apartment, the beautiful views of the valley and about the neighbours. I've described the apartment to him several times in my enthusiasm; it is square, well actually it's not square, not many buildings are in this part of the world. When I first arrived, I kept moving the table and chairs wondering why they always looked crooked until on closer inspection I realised the wall was oblique and I laughed out loud.

The main room has a sofa at one end and a small shelf unit and, as I said, a table and chairs; all along the side opposite the front door is the kitchen with a sink unit, hob and hood and numerous pans and saucepans hanging under the top units and in front of the tiles. More shelves to the right and a large lattice window by the front door and behind the sofa, so it is bright and cheery. Two bedrooms and a bed that creeks every time I move, a single wardrobe and a small tatty chest of drawers; it was transformed when I put my Indian silk cloth over it. There is another small lattice window on the wall opposite my bed and three bookshelves next to it. I was relieved to find thee having brought a few books and my writing gear with me; much to the surprise of all the kind men who struggled with my suitcases from Beckenham to Valle Gran Rey.

Peter is excited about his ensuing trip, well as excited as he can be, he doesn't often express himself and when he does it's a low-key affair. I am the complete opposite, demonstrative in fact, and I talk with my hands; some friends say I must be of Mediterranean origin. My facial expressions are quite animated at times, and I have been known to talk too rather too much.

It was a wonderful evening. I always appreciate good company and good food, but now stormy skies hang over the valley, rain is falling and being blown in sheets across the ravines. Brenda drives us home and the further up the valley we climb, the more cloud and rain appears. It can be very cloudy to the back of our apartments and sometimes you can see the clouds swirling higher up, at the same time you can walk down the valley and it is brilliant sunshine. We have the best of both worlds in Casa de la Seda, plenty of sun and strong breezes to cool the high temperatures, which in July and August is a welcome relief.

"Peter's arriving from waterlogged England in the morning so I hope it's not raining tomorrow."

"The island needs all the rain it can get Geraldine." Brenda says in her best schoolteacher voice and instantly I want to crawl under a rock and hide for having the audacity to complain about the weather.

"If you go walking after a downpour you see new colourful plants in between the rocks." I'm keeping quiet in case I put my foot in it again, but I'm taking it all in. "And when we have a storm and there's torrential rain, waterfalls cascade down the mountains on all sides of the valley. It's a magnificent sight, then as the rocks dry out you can hear tremendous cracks like great claps of thunder."

I can't wait to see and hear these phenomena.

Chapter Four

Throughout the centuries
humans have fashioned their existence,
the genius, the leader and the masses
have created a past – making history,
but history can be fashioned,
by the scribe or recorder of the day.

Pedro is kindly taking me to San Sebastian to meet Peter, who is arriving this morning. Lilly is sitting in the back of the truck practising her Spanish with her colourful schoolbook on her lap. Over and over, she is repeating her words while I look at the thick green forest of The Garajonay National Park. Alto de Garajonay is the highest point of the island, 1,487 metres above sea level. La Gomera, being very small, means it slopes sharply towards the sea. The National Park, a vestige of the Tertiary period no less, was declared a national park in 1982 and was listed in 1986 by UNESCO, as a world heritage of mankind, covering almost 10% of the island.

The highest regions of Garajonay Mountain are covered by the forest where prehistoric vegetation is nurtured by water from its numerous springs. The name Garajonay comes from an ancient legend. Gara a beautiful young lady lived on La Gomera, and Jonay was a young man from Tenerife who arrived here on a raft of goatskins filled with air. They met and fell in love. Their families, especially Gara's father, did not approve and forbade them to see each other. The two lovers fled to the highest point of the island taking their own lives with a double-edged wooden stake, by sharpening it at both ends and supporting it between their two chests. How romantic, and it sounds familiar too; maybe that's where Shakespeare got the idea for Romeo and Juliet.

36

All of a sudden one of the gigantic roques comes into view and looms on the misty landscape. They are solidified lava monoliths and with cloud gathering around them they look mysterious; my imagination starts to run wild.

Solidified lava monoliths

A monument stands near Los Roques. There was a fire in the valley below in nineteen-eighty-four and many people stood and watched as the fire fighters struggled to put it out. The strong winds changed direction suddenly, as they do on this island, and so did the fire. Twenty-one people were killed, including the Civil Governor of

Tenerife province. Sadly, he put politics before safety. It's poignant standing reading all the names on the memorial.

La Gomera is a small island, but it conceals an ecological treasure and few places in the world have so much natural wealth. On the central high plateau, which is nearly always under the protection of a shroud of mist, lies a unique and thick evergreen forest; contrasting sharply with the arid landscapes on some lower areas of the island. The height of the mountains stops the clouds, which are pushed by prevailing winds, until they unload their moisture in a unique phenomenon, horizontal rain; therefore, a foggy veil extends over the lush vegetation. Trees grow to 500 metres often in strange and twisted forms, a genuine rain forest.

The National Park was created precisely to save the ecosystem, the largest and most complete sample of Canary Rainforest Laurisilva. In the park the climate is extremely regular and only the rainfall during the winter months brings about any change. A sea of clouds stretches out across the park. The rainforest is the only surviving example of the woodlands, which once covered the margins of the Mediterranean Sea several million years ago. I'm half expecting to see a Tyrannosaurus Rex appear.

On my first day on La Gomera I missed a lot of this scenery as I was feeling tired and queasy, but today I can enjoy it. Low cloud and mist are swirling all around us giving the landscape a magical feel. My father used to say I had my head in the clouds, well now his words have come true.

In the ninth century, B.C. Homer, wrote about the Canary Islands and called them the 'Elysian Fields' and I can see why. This wonderful island is made for people who want to escape into the lush forests, the beautiful ravines, and the sweeping green valleys. It is a dramatic and varied landscape with scenery sculptured by the oceans; steep and enormous cliffs take you back to different times. An island with vibrant energy and a calming atmosphere where you can soak it up and revitalise yourself as a visitor or better still live here. La Gomera has an ambience all of its own. I seemed to have entered the magic of its soul as so many others have done previously.

The higher villages have been regenerated by the return of 'the sons of La Gomera' who left the island in the sixties and seventies in droves to work elsewhere. Many of the young people did not want to work on the land and it was a depressing time. Fortunately, many of them returned to their beautiful home with their hard-earned money to invest in tourism and in the villages. Over the past few years, it has improved communications and economic aspects which it deserves. This will bring benefits to this much loved island but not too many changes, I hope. Recently I heard a young man from Tenerife say we are behind the times on Gomera. "Thank goodness", I said to myself, this is why people love this beautiful and unspoilt island. Parts are still wild and untamed, a bit like me my son and daughter would probably say.

Tourism has increased and has obviously brought benefits, but it is still easy to find small silent places where Mother Nature reigns. There is peace, tranquillity, and beauty to be found on La Gomera. The palm tree law only allows buildings to be three stories high and no higher than a palm tree. I have seen some huge palm trees on the island, and I've also witnessed a few four storey buildings springing up, which is not too bad. I can't think of anything worse than finding a tower block on the horizon; luckily the terrain is such that there never will be enormous tourist complexes here.

The many German residents I meet love La Gomera and do not want to rush back to their homeland and I feel the same way about England. I certainly don't miss the ever-increasing discussions and some of the ridiculous arguments about political correctness. I wholeheartedly agree we must not use derogatory words or phrases that may upset and insult people, but England has now swung too far in the opposite direction. I do not miss the inflated prices in most of the shops and the general rudeness of some English people either. Certainly, I don't mean all English people but at one time we were known as such polite folk. Maybe the weather has something to do with it. England can be grey and full of gloom, but you usually find when the sun comes out people start to speak to each other again.

There are some things I miss about England, besides my children of course, the countryside is diverse and beautiful; unfortunately, the weather is also diverse, and it definitely affects people's moods. Having always been friendly and out-going I would naturally speak to people in the street and say hello to strangers. Why is it when you do this some folk, look at you as if you have suddenly grown two heads and others want to have you sectioned?

Sadly, I cannot receive BBC Radio 4 or the World Service because of the topography of the island. Mornings won't be the same without John Humphreys. How I'm going to live without Nicholas Parsons and 'Just a Minute', 'The News Quiz' and 'Sorry I haven't a clue' with the hilariously funny Humphrey Littleton, I do not know? People like Paul Merton, Barry Cryer, Tim

Brook-Taylor, Clement Freud, and Graeme Garden, to name but a few used to send me into fits of giggles with their fast wit. Listening to these programmes on the car radio, I would go into absolute hysterics, and I often received strange looks when sitting at traffic lights.

A sea of fir trees in front of us reminds me I have always wanted to spend Christmas abroad to get away from the commercialism in England at this time of year. It's refreshing to walk into the supermacados in Valle Gran Rey and not have Christmas cards, decorations, large boxes of sweets and chocolates, stockings and gifts taking up every available space in the shop. It bugs me in England when the first sign of Christmas appears in September and in extreme cases August, when people are still trying to relax on their holidays from the everyday pressures of life.

It always strikes me as strange that most people buy enormous amounts of food then proceed to stuff themselves for the short Christmas holiday; knowing waistlines will expand, but purses and wallets will not. This Christmas will certainly be a strange one. We'll have a Christmas dinner of sorts, in the hope that someone from England will send us a box of sage and onion stuffing and a Christmas pudding. This will hopefully be followed by a swim in the sea, a leisurely rest on the beach and a fiesta or two.

In my enthusiasm I start to talk too much, and I can read the expression on Pedro's face as he tries to concentrate on the winding mountain roads and the sharp bends. Sitting with mouth shut tight I continue to admire the verdant and undulating terrain. Still feeling slightly queasy on this journey, I wonder if I will ever get used to travelling across the island; it's a bit like being on a helter-skelter in places.

The mountains are brown and dry on this side of the island, but the pretty town of San Sebastian is now in sight so there's not much further to go. It is the capital of the island and has 7000 inhabitants. It has a well-equipped harbour for sailing boats in The Canaries. Maybe I will meet a rich handsome sailor and we can spend our evenings on his enormous yacht, watching the sun set over the ocean drinking large gin and tonics. Sorry, I was daydreaming again, something I've done since I was a child.

Sans Sebastian Town

San Sebastian being the capital of the island means it has a history of fights, sieges, and adventures. At the end of the 15th century Christopher Columbus anchored here for a few days; he was on his way to the New World and many people mistakenly think that Columbus sailed directly from Portugal. It is from this important event in history, of which La Gomera is terribly proud, it gets its name, 'Isla Colombina'

Columbus knew Beatrice de Bobadilla who was a young widow and governor of the island. He installed himself in the Castle de San Sebastian, where Beatrice made her home. The only wing remaining is the Torre del Conde (Tower of the Count), a monument which still stands and there are some remains of the admiral's visit. Beatrice made sure Columbus had plenty of provisions at the best prices, so his ships were stuffed with meats, flour and cheeses and the men collected wood and water. The day before departure the men went to confess their sins and hear mass in the Church of the Asuncion. Columbus left La Gomera on the morning of 6th September 1492 for his expedition to America. It was the last place he stayed at until he reached the new continent.

The Torre del Conde was part of an ancient fortress founded around 1450. Now as you enter the tower you climb the worn, but solid wood stairs. Looking through the gun turrets, as they would have done centuries ago when trying to protect themselves against the numerous invaders, I can see the port. The floors of the fortress are worn and there are oak beams as you make your way up to the top, where there's an opening onto a wooden ledge. The tower itself is not too impressive but there is a wonderful collection of old maps and aerial views of the Canary Archipelago. There are also some excellent sketches of San Sebastian.

The tower is now surrounded by a beautiful park, where the locals take their children for picnics and lovers sit under the trees. There's also a wonderful amphitheatre with stone steps curving in a semi-circle for the audience to sit on. Unfortunately, it doesn't look as if it's been used for some time as there are rather a lot of weeds growing in the cracks. What a shame, I think as I take centre stage.

Church of the Asuncion

Church of the Asuncion was first constructed in the 15th century. It lays back and in front of it is a small square with a few trees where the locals shade themselves. It is still enveloped by cobblestone streets and little white houses. There is an impressive late Gothic door and as you enter the church a mantle of peace and calm envelopes you. I wonder if the locals would object to a heathen sitting in their church, especially one who talks to spirit people.

The Church of the Asuncion has been subjected to different reconstructions through the time of the Renaissance, the Baroque and all the epochs. On my visit I saw and admired the mural called 'Capilla del Pilar'. It depicts the heroic event of the defence of the Villa and the island against the English naval attacks, by the pirate Charles Windon and is well worth a look. Stopping in San Sebastian, the sailors and conquerors would visit the church to ask for luck in their adventures and they would pray before going off to kill other human beings. It's strange that whenever there is a conflict or a war people across the globe pray to the same God and they all think he is on their side; well, that's my opinion anyway

In the 16th century San Sebastian was a call port and through here passed the most famous sailors and conquerors. Towards the end of the 16th century, and throughout the 17th century, Gomera was under constant attack and many inhabitants had to flee to the interior of the island to find protection; from this time until modern times, the Gomeras have emigrated to South America, and there is a strong link to this part of the world.

I'm looking forward to seeing Peter again. We continue to wind down the mountain road towards San Sebastian. It is not such a clear day, so the view of mount Teide is less spectacular. We enter the port and I'm looking forward to sharing the apartment with a friend. I love my own company but being in a completely new environment is an entirely different feeling for me. Not being able to reach for the phone and chat to my friends as I did in England sometimes makes me feel isolated, but it certainly saves on the phone bill. Fortunately, this feeling only lasts a few minutes and soon I'm positive and happy again; all the same it will be good to have a friend around, I hope.

Pedro parks and while we're waiting, he fiddles with his old engine while Lilly and I scan the many passengers coming down the steps of the Fred Olsen Express. We see Peter and wave. I don't know if we expect him to wave back with luggage in both hands, but he has a grin on his face.

After the long journey and the excitement of the day Peter and I find ourselves sitting quietly on the terrace admiring the valley. Most nights, before he arrived, I would sit for long stretches of time in the silence. It is marvellous when you link with nature and it's a good form of relaxation and meditation. Peter switches the light off so we can see more clearly, and I'm surprised I didn't think of it before; sometimes I am rather slow. There appears before our eyes an awesome sight … an indigo sky adorned with millions of stars, like crystals winking in the night. No sound apart from the crickets, the intermittent rustle in the undergrowth and the occasional unwelcome noise of a car.

There are only four lights around the Los Reyes Church on the left and a few lamp posts to the far right in El Guro, so there's not much light pollution. Streetlights have been an addition to the island in recent years. Before they were introduced, people used to walk around holding glass jars with a candle burning inside. I have been told it was a beautiful sight and a wonderful time to live on La Gomera and I'm sure I would have loved it, being the romantic type.

El Guro, on the right hand side of the valley, is a pretty sight indeed. Houses are built on the terraces and there is an abundance of palm trees towering over the buildings. To get to their homes the inhabitants have to climb hundreds of steps, twisting backwards and forwards up the mountainside. I would not like to have to walk up these every day, though I could end up looking like a stick insect. One of Annabelle's friends lives at the top of this village, and she said when she first did a big shop, with a neighbour, they had a few carrier bags between them and it was hard going; they didn't even get halfway when they collapsed on the steps in fits of giggles, with their shopping all around them. Anita says it is such a beautiful place to live it's worth it. She bought what is called a ruine and there are many on the island. The stone house consists of two rooms and one of these was for cheese making. It's incredible to think that people on the island used to live in these tiny homes with their animals; I can't imagine sharing my home with a goat.

Chapter Five

Like a swan in restless flight
we thrash about,
but when we find the inner peace we truly desire,
then we, the swan, will glide on a calmer river,
regardless of the ripples.

Farmed terraces

Every day I notice something different about the valley and I never tire of looking. Swinging my eyes to the left as it curves round, I see the abundant terraces. Looking past them, I see the horses being trained down near the stables. I love to sit here and watch their antics and listen to their protestations as they neigh loudly. New stables are being built to replace the old ones. Past these and coming into view are the steps up to the attractive little church, Eta de Los Reyes, sitting in the slopes. Underneath the church the trees and bushes growing look as though they are about to tumble down onto the thick bamboo below. What a soothing sight it is when it's lit up at night. It's a landmark in the valley and is a peaceful area.

My neighbour Paulette has her music blaring out and although I like her choice of songs, I sometimes wish she would play it a few decibels lower. Today I need peace, so I walk over to the church. It's a rough and winding path lined with banana trees and thick vegetation. I always stop halfway to look through the great palm fronds at the ocean in the distance. There is no one to be seen as I continue to walk then climb the many steep and uneven stone steps to the church. The silence is welcoming so I sit on a bench, shut my eyes, and soak up the atmosphere.

About ten minutes have passed and I'm feeling rejuvenated already, but a large black dog has appeared at one end of the church forecourt and it's barking and growling menacingly. Where are all the German walkers when you want them?

Sitting frozen on the bench I now long for people to appear and I would do anything to be back in my apartment listening to Paulette's ear-splitting music. Chased by an Alsatian at the age of twelve resulted in me being terrified of our four legged friends for years afterwards. In my late twenties I remember walking round the block rather than walk past a big noisy dog. It was a general election, and I was supposed to be chasing up the last minute voters; well, I did not return to that particular street, and I never found out how many votes we may have lost because of it. Thank God this big black dog realises he can't bully me, so he skulks off. Now I can make my escape, slowly at first, then reaching the stone steps on the left side of the church, I jump down two at a time.

However, despite this isolated incident a strange thing has happened since I've been here all the neighbourhood dogs seem to converge on me. I must be sending out doggy 'vibes' as they climb the steps to my apartment to say hello. Apart from the angry dog incident at the church, I'm not usually scared any more. Kuro, Lara, Lunar and Torrie all come up at different times of the day when I'm sitting on the terrace; they flop themselves down next to my chair when I'm writing and apart from wanting the occasional stroke they lie contentedly in the sun. It's hard to believe I sit calmly next to them without breaking out in a cold sweat and thanks to them I've cured my fear of dogs.

It's the Tuesday after Peter arrived, and Bernie and Ann have invited us to go out with them in their car. We set off to Chipude and El Cercado, two villages higher up the mountain; they are called the 1000 metre villages, and this is where the potteries are. Two of the local women are sitting outside kneading clay and making their pots the way they have been making them for the past 500 years; not these particular ladies of course. They do not use a potter's wheel but cleverly form the clay into all sorts of things without one. They use furnaces with wood and the secrecy of the mixture of grounds and sands to obtain a plastic mud is jealously guarded.

Peter is holding two painted mugs and I'm admiring a jug to match when I hear a gasp. Turning round I see him catching a mug and he is holding the handle in his other hand, with a look of surprise on his face. It must have been loose, but the potter is shrewd, and she is speaking very fast. We look at her blankly until we realise, she is trying to say we have to pay for it. We shake our heads, and she decides to let the matter go, looking slightly peeved. She soon cheers up and smiles broadly when a coach-load of German tourists arrive, and we make a quick get-away.

We are now making for Santiago and although the sun is hot there is some low cloud as we climb higher. Forte Lazo is coming into sight, and I can see why it is sometimes called, 'Table Mountain'; it is an eroded volcanic vent with a vast summit plateau. With the arrival of the Spaniards, it was used as a retreat from the attackers. It often has white feathery cloud swirling beneath the flat top, and it is a steep ascent but popular.

Ann unfurls her map of La Gomera while Bernie is concentrating on the winding roads and hairpin bends. We are looking for the wild dragon tree, El Drago de Alajero. On Tenerife there is a dragon tree which is supposed to be 2000-3000 years old, but the one we're looking for is a mere 1000 years old. The sap in a dragon tree turns red on contact with the air and is called dragon blood, hence the name. The Guanche (early natives) used it as ointment and to embalm their dead. In Venice it was used by wealthy ladies as an ingredient in a dye to make their hair golden. Florentine masons poured the liquid dragon's blood onto marble to stain it red and it was also used by Italian 17th century violinists as a rich varnish for their instruments. It was thought to have supernatural powers and was burnt as an incense to obstruct the work of witches.

Brenda told us the dragon tree is just off the road and we can't miss it, but we have. It is not well sign posted; maybe they don't want too many tourists finding it. I'm disappointed as a tree as old as that will have a phenomenal amount of energy and I wanted to give it a hug. Maybe it's just as well, if Bernie had seen me embracing a tree, he might have had a funny turn.

We find the new airport at Santiago. It's a beautiful spacious building inside but it turned into a bit of a white elephant and had to close. Now it has been re-opened. It's bright and tastefully decorated but it's only used for short flights with small by-planes to Gran Canaria and Tenerife; as we drive away, we can see why the runway is built straight up from the side of the mountain and is extremely short.

Santiago is a pretty harbour town and white houses of all shapes are dotted along the valley road to the beach. There are few beautiful villas and one of them, I'm told, belongs to, Ronald Biggs, the great train robber. About halfway down we find the Hotel Jardin Tecina which boasts three swimming pools and five restaurants. We have been told we can use one of the restaurants and a sea water swimming pool downstairs, but the restaurants upstairs look more to our liking. We cheekily sit down, looking like residents and the waiter seems to be convinced; I just hope he doesn't ask for our room numbers. Lunch is well prepared and delicious and it's so good not to be rushed. Three hours have passed, and we have not stopped talking, eating, and laughing. Now it's time for a swim.

Ann is not too keen on the lift shaft which is built into an enormous black cliff and comes out at another restaurant down below with a swimming pool. I can't wait to jump in so immediately I start stripping off. I do have my swimming costume on underneath of course as I don't want to frighten the hotel guests away.

After swimming for half an hour, I have the strong taste of salt in my mouth. It's not just to give the guests the authentic taste of the ocean its actually recycled seawater. I know you're not supposed to swallow it, but I can't help it when a poser, resembling a triangle on legs, steams past me looking like he's swimming for the Olympics. In need of a large gin and tonic to take the taste away I climb out.

A few minutes later, happily lounging by the pool with the others, I notice the triangle on legs has gone to lie on the sun bed next to his girlfriend. She looks like she should be on a roasting spit and I'm sure she's been cooked on both sides. She reminds me of my sister Lynn who has always been a sun-worshipper.

We arrive home and the evening air is refreshing. The sunset is exceptional, and the sky looks like it's on fire. We don't get to watch it for long as Brenda wants to borrow Peter. Most of the houses on La Gomera have roof terraces for their water tanks and sometimes washing machines. It's where they hang up washing, dry chillies and sometimes grow grapevines. Brenda has her washing machine situated on the roof terrace and it has to be replaced. She needs a couple of men and as Bernie and another friend Danny, who is staying with her, and Peter are available she has asked them if they can haul it onto the roof. I can't imagine how they are going to achieve it with a wooden ladder and some ropes but then I'm not a very practical person.

Ann, Brenda, Pia, and myself watch the men tie the rope round the machine; I never did learn how to tie sailor's knots and I admire anyone who can. Bernie and Danny are on the roof and Bernie says it resembles B&Q, so he moves a few things then shouts down to Peter. The washing machine is hauled up with Peter underneath it. Halfway up it slides away from the ladder nearly smashing into the bathroom window. Peter pulls the machine back onto the ladder and it's hovering precariously above his head. Brenda is wearing a worried look Ann is biting her lips and Pia is giving out the orders; she reminds me of my own daughter at that age. Peter decides to lift the ladder up so they can slide the washing machine along the rungs, and I can't believe the whole operation has taken only a few minutes. It can take me five minutes to open a can of tomatoes and invariable I manage to splatter the contents onto my clean clothes.

Chapter Six

Perfect climate,
scenery sculptured by the elements,
a floating wheel
on the vast Atlantic Ocean,
a piece of Homers'
'Elysian Fields'.

Three weeks I have been in Valle Gran Rey and already the journey from England is becoming vague and I feel I belong on the 'Fortune Islands.' Today is Bernie and Ann's last day so we are going for a meal. They have all been to visit Brenda's eldest daughter Chloe at Tenerife University. She dislikes Tenerife and misses La Gomera a great deal. It's strange to think that as Chloe starts her university life on another island, so my nephew begins his university life at Loughborough in England. Simultaneously at this time of year youngsters in many countries are beginning a new experience with excitement; most of them will have memories to treasure for the rest of their lives.

Once again Brenda's choice of restaurant is good; a local Spanish restaurant called San Jose at La Playa. The proprietor and the staff are extremely friendly, and the food is excellent. Our waiter finds out I am living here and insists I order my meal in Spanish. I love their chicken in salsa and can never resist the 'Papas Arugadas', which are new potatoes cooked in their skins and almost boiled dry, so they have a crunchy coating of salt. I just hope my limited Spanish has enabled me to order the correct meal but there's only one way to find out wait and see what turns up.

The meal was absolutely wonderful and the atmosphere in San Jose is perfect. Afterwards Brenda takes us to a Bar; one of the few bars owned by an Englishman and he's been living here for several years. Recognising the accent, I realise he is from somewhere near London, and it turns out to be Essex.

All of a sudden, our table is being extended and two more English people join us for a drink. A man called Alan, with a salt and pepper beard and a twinkle in his eye, sits next to me. He was born in South Africa and still has the accent even though he has lived in Wales for nine years with his partner Jill. He loved Wales and says it has some of the best scenery in Britain. But the main reason he came to La Gomera was because of the enormous amount of rain in Wales and the continuous lack of sun. Wanting somewhere to enjoy the rest of his life, where he could relax, and slowdown was a priority. Alan tells me he bought his house on a handshake and even the locals were surprised when he moved in rent free for four months while the paperwork was going through.

Jill was a nurse for the National Health Service and now she works for a private insurance company; she flies home with patients who are ill or dying. She has to nurse them or in some cases keep them alive until they reach their destination. The insurance company pays all her expenses. For the first time in her life, she is overpaid and under-worked instead of being underpaid and overworked. Living up in the mountains on this beautiful island can't be bad either.

Alan and Jill live in Los Asivignos, Hermigua, which is north-west of La Gomera. It's on the edge of El Cedro, the beautiful forest covering the higher regions of the mountains; it has some of the most stunning scenery on the island. Alan tells me he is a potato farmer, but I can't help laughing because he doesn't look like a potato farmer whatever a potato farmer looks like; he insists he is serious. He says it does not pay well so he has the odd bit of building work as well. The spectacular scenery is one of the reasons Alan wants to live out his days here; not a bad recommendation. They both enjoy their surroundings and they do not need a vast amount of money or lots of material things to be happy.

A few days later Peter and I decide it is about time we did some serious walking, so we set off for a mountain hike. We don't intend to go too far, so I'm not carrying a big bag of supplies. Walking down into the barranco (deep ravine) and then up to Los Reyes church is not too difficult for me and it's effortless for Peter. We pass a few houses where access looks extremely difficult. It must be arduous when the owners of these homes need to bring up something heavy. How on earth would you get a washing machine up here for instance? The next thing we come across is some sort of hoist which is the answer to my question. Wooden frames house the winches, but it looks extremely rickety. Supplies are put in the cage and hoisted up but a washing machine? Apparently, the amount of wine, beer, spirits, and food needed for the Christmas celebrations at Los Reyes Church is phenomenal and it all gets hoisted up via this winch. I can hardly wait!

Passed the church we walk across a small gorge which has had numerous rock-falls. Following the arrows on the goat trail we notice the scenery changing below us to a forest of bamboo and thick palm trees. It is green and luscious. A donkey is staring up at me and blinking in the sunlight; he has harnesses on and is obviously used to transport building materials. I immediately feel sorry for him having to carry such heavy weights, but the locals would think me silly and sentimental. Gomeras have been using donkeys in this way for many centuries.

The condition of the donkey's hooves is sometimes appalling although it does not happen so much these days. They are not always filed down and can curve round and cause much discomfort. You cannot move to a foreign land and expect to change what has been for many generations. However, when my neighbour Brenda arrived a few years ago she was so upset by what she saw she started to file the donkey's hooves herself. She showed the locals how to do it because in those days there was no blacksmith in the valley. I must say though that this donkey looks well cared for.

The view of the ravines is spectacular the higher we climb and it's interesting to see Valle Gran Rey from a different perspective. I can certainly feel my muscles working. Peter is speeding ahead, and I have to remind him to slow down. He's always been extra slim, and he can move much faster than I can. Another good reason for stopping is to admire the beautiful views, well, that's my excuse anyway.

Some of the old stone shacks we see were lived in at one time. In England they would probably be called cottages as anything, however small, gets labelled a cottage and sold at exorbitant prices. We climb off the path and clamber over rocks to investigate one of the ruined shacks. Stonewalls were built into the mountain and they consisted of just two rooms. You can see evidence of a cooking area with bits of old crockery and ashes and goat herders may have used it recently.

The Guanche, original natives of La Gomera, were tall and sturdy with blue eyes and fair hair and they lived in caves many centuries ago; there is still evidence of these dwelling places. They used to bury their dead in the caves and mummies have been found. One mummy was found in a cave in the Canary Islands in recent years and it was discovered by scientists to be similar to the Egyptian mummies, although it does not seem conceivable for the Egyptians to have travelled to The Canaries in those days, it now seems a possibility.

We pass a pretty little house also built into the mountain and wondering how precarious it is living in these properties, with the ever-present possibility of a rock fall, I stop and look. It has artistic pictures on the door and well-kept potted plants resting in gaps in the wall along the front of the house. It's isolated and quaint and I have a strong feeling a writer or artist lives here. The original building looks like it's been improved, and it has a low sloping roof. Peace and tranquillity surely exist in this obscure place and must be enjoyed by the occupier. Peace is necessary to me, but I don't know if I could be this isolated. Being on my own certainly suits me but I also I like to have people around me; I am a sociable animal. This is when I need discipline to sit at my computer and ignore the outside world, but I do enjoy writing. Some people think if you work at home that you are not working at all; fortunately, most of my friends do understand. My daughter used to tell everyone who telephoned that I was out, when I was working on a new chapter of the novel that took me nearly seven years to finish. It certainly helps not having the little square box sitting in the corner of the room and it's incredible to think I have not watched Coronation Street for five weeks.

We decide to take the easy path, which comes out at the village of Chele. Before we walk through the village, I notice a 'For Sale' sign a little higher up and I can now see a ruine. It's not in good condition and the sign is broken and obviously old.

"How the hell is anyone supposed to get up there?" I ask Peter.

"God knows," he replies, straining to see if there is a path. "Looks very overgrown but there must have been access at one time." I fully expect him to climb up and prove his point.

"Well, I wouldn't fancy climbing up there every day."

"If you lived there, you'd get used to it Gel."

"Phew not me," I lose interest and started to walk on, but Peter soon catches up.

Walking through the village of Chele is pleasant and it is definitely a more affluent area as the houses are much bigger. Something I greatly admire about Gomera is no home ever looks the same and there are no little boxes to be seen, but of course they don't have so many people to house as we do in England. Some of these houses are huge and have the most beautiful terraces looking down into the deep ravine. Sweeping my eyes up the valley I realise that Valle Gran Rey is one of the prettiest places I have ever seen.

Some parts of the island remind me of Cyprus with all the banana plantations: high cliffs hugging little bays resemble Cornwall and Scotland: rolling hills remind me of Wales. I've heard people say parts of Gomera resemble of India, Venezuela, and Hawaii. It's not surprising as this island has such a diverse terrain, making it scenic and interesting especially for the many walkers who visit. Sometimes I wish I was a proficient walker because it is said unless you walk all over the island, some of the assents are incredible, you do not see half of it. I'll just have to make do with the other half, won't I.

We decide to go back along the easy path so we can climb a small gorge beside a house. I clamber up after Peter thoroughly enjoying it as I'm still a child at heart and I like to explore. Parts of the gorge look precarious and at one point I mistakenly grab a prickly pear, ouch! I'll be pulling out tiny needles from my hand for the rest of the day and it's surprising how they hurt. We finally reach a path which we had not realised runs parallel with the gorge behind the house. Now we know why the man of the house is giving us such a funny look; he must think we are idiots. Oh well, I enjoyed the scramble up the gorge which wasn't dangerous, and it was good exercise.

Carrying on up the mountain path is invigorating but I have to stop every now and again to catch my breath. It means I can admire the scenery and view the valley from different aspects. We can see our apartment block in the distance and people down below look like ants. Also, I want to let the experienced walkers pass me as the Germans take their walking seriously and they are super fit. The last thing I want is for them to see my chest heaving they might throw me to the floor and give me emergency resuscitation.

Finally, for me anyway, we reach a small buff and I'm making myself comfortable on a large flat rock with a panoramic view of the ravines. Once again, I can see the ocean at the bottom of the valley in the distance and it gives me the sensation of being suspended in mid-air.

A young couple stop to ask Peter the way and he points to a path winding further up to the top which is almost hidden in amongst the cacti. They hesitate, then decide to go for it, so if youngsters waver, I can't have done too bad at the age of forty-eight. I can swim a mile, but I'm not used to walking in the mountains; maybe I'll be rid of this spare tyre soon. The diet gurus say if you can 'pinch an inch of fat' you need to lose weight, with me it's more like a handful and I long for the day when my jeans do not leave a vicious looking red weal around my waist.

Peter decides to climb higher to take yet more photographs because he's happiest when his finger is pressing the small button on top of his camera. Sometimes he reminds me of a Japanese tourist.

I'm contented sitting on my flat rock and I'm breathing normally again while taking in the clean mountain air. There's no one around so I'll have a meditation to replenish my energy. It doesn't matter if the odd walker comes close because I can detach myself and be at one with my surroundings; I just hope they don't ask me the time and expect an answer.

Gomeras in a popular local restaurant

Chapter Seven

Swimming in the sea
unconstrained like the seagulls
bobbing up and down
on cool oscillating waves
surrounding La Gomera.

I thought I had left miserable bus drivers behind in England but two of the regular bus drivers here look like they'd rather be anywhere other than driving a bus on sun drenched La Gomera. This driver is one of them and when I smile sweetly it only seems to aggravate him. He has no manners and when I say gracias, he just manages a grunt. If they are trying to encourage tourists to the island, they should have a word in his 'shell like' he could easily frighten off visitors with one look.

There are four buses a day in Valle Gran Rey, but the bus drivers are having some sort of dispute with the taxi drivers and as a result they've not been running for a couple of days. Today is Sunday and Peter and I are watching another beautiful sunset. The last bus should have gone at six thirty, but another bus has arrived, and it is now twenty minutes past seven. We both agree that maybe the dispute has resulted in an extra bus being put on which means we can watch the sunset and catch a bus home afterwards. This gives me that wonderful warm glow I had as a child when dad bought us all a bag of chips on the way home from a day's outing. It's a shame to have to miss the laborious walk up to the apartment, but there's always tomorrow.

The following day Brenda has arranged for us to meet the principle of the language school, which is in La Calera, a hilly village with lots of little alleyways in between the houses; there are a few lovely shops too. My favourite restaurant in La Calera is El Mirador and has a wonderful view of the ocean. I can sit with a snack and a large bottle of water for a couple of hours, relaxing, watching the waves, and reading my book. In England I'd probably be shooed out of the restaurant, so I could vacate my table for the more serious eaters.

View of La Calera

La Calera is nearer to the beach but is still far enough away from the hubbub for you to find solitude and the view of the bottom of the valley is glorious. There are more banana plantations, and you can see the beaches and the rugged coastline below. It's a captivating sight especially as you watch the waves crashing onto the rocks.

We have been waiting thirty minutes for Maria and it's unusual for a teacher to be late. We were supposed to meet her here at one thirty and it's now 2 o'clock. Peter is restless. He doesn't really want to learn a new language, even though it would make his time on Gomera more interesting, so we decide to visit El Mirador instead of hanging around any longer. Evelyn, one of the waitresses, is very helpful when I practise my Spanish and she often writes phrases or words down on scraps of paper for me. If she gets impatient with my early attempts at her native language, she doesn't show it; she has the sweetest smile and disposition.

We eat a somewhat calorific snack followed by a lovely afternoon walk home from La Calera. The road is not as steep so it's kinder on my thighs.

Lilly has come down to visit us tonight and has decided to stay for dinner. Its eight o'clock and I think it's too late for a six-year old to be eating but she doesn't seem to think it's that late. Suddenly the light switches on in my brain we should have put the clocks back. Peter and I have a good giggle when we think of the series of mishaps over the last two days. No wonder the photocopying lady wasn't in the Kodac shop yesterday it wasn't five thirty it was four thirty. And what we thought was an extra bus at seven thirty was really the six thirty. The reason Maria never arrived at the school was because our watches were an hour wrong. Mystery solved!

Before you think we're utterly stupid remember we have no television and the radio is in Spanish, plus, I have not bought a newspaper for over a week so unlike the people in England we had no reminders. I apologise to Brenda as she set up the meeting with Maria, so we could be interviewed in view of enrolling on a Spanish course. She laughs and says she did the same thing when she arrived thirteen years ago. I have no way of telling whether she is saying this to help me feel better or not, but it does make me feel less of an airhead.

My son, Joe, has come to stay for a few days and I can imagine what he will say when I tell him the story of the clocks not going back. He cannot believe how long it took to reach my apartment from the time he left the plane at Tenerife. I have warned my family and friends that it might only take four hours on the plane but the whole trip takes the best part of a day; with the journey to and from Valle Gran Rey Joe only has three days left.

I'm glad I prepared a Bolognese for dinner which is Joe's favourite. It was Joe's favourite. We were ravenous when we arrived home and twirled spaghetti around our forks with much anticipation. But after one mouthful I knew something was wrong and the look on Joe's face was confirmation enough.

"Aw mum, this is disgusting," he says and looks like he's going to spit it out but thinks better of it.

"Yes, it is pretty gruesome." I take another mouthful out of curiosity but soon regret it, "Yuk, that's the first and the last time I buy minced beef on La Gomera."

"Mum, believe me, this is not minced beef."

"No, you're right, I think it must be from an old goat."

"Yeah mum, a very old goat," and we end up laughing despite our disappointment.

The next morning a trip to the beach is obviously a good idea because I want to laze on the sand and read my book in peace. Knowing how difficult it will be for Joe to lie on the beach for a long it doesn't surprise me when after only a few minutes he is looking for something to do. I groan when he persistently disturbs me, and I give up trying to read one of Bill Bryson's hilariously funny travel books; instead, I try to keep my son amused as I used to do when he was small.

We try beach tennis, but he laughingly says I'm useless. The ball keeps going in the wrong direction and in the end floats off on the crest of a wave, so dropping the bats we end up in the sea ourselves. My two have always been water babies, like their mum, and we jump the waves like a pair of kids. Not paying attention and forgetting about the winter tides a large wave catches me unexpectedly and knocks me violently under the water. Rising out of the sea I gasp for air and realise I have a bruised bum; only I could manage to fall on a small rock. Joe finds it highly amusing and I'm so glad he's no longer bored.

The days have flown by. Yesterday we went on an all-day boat trip to see the dolphins. We did see a few swimming around the boat but not as many as we would have liked. The boat was comfortable, and it was quite calm to begin with but soon the sky clouded over, the wind started to blow, and the sea became choppy. Loving every minute of it I hung over the side of the boat with the spray splashing on my face; unfortunately, the swell got bigger, and a few people went the colour of mushy peas. The captain announced it was too rough for us to continue to the north of the island which was disappointing. I wanted Joe to see Los Organos which is a cliff of basalt and actually looks like giant organ pipes. Twenty metres wide and eighty metres high it is an impressive sight.

There was some unusual scenery though and an enormous outcrop of rocks with the waves smashing onto them. The captain obviously knowing the waters well seemed to steer rather close to these huge rocks. This made some of the passengers feel worse as they watched goggle eyed and then lurched over the side to empty the contents of their stomachs. Watching the large waves meant I was standing near them, and I just avoided being covered as the wind blew in my direction. A few passengers were relieved when the captain turned the boat round and we headed back to calmer waters.

We dropped anchor off a quiet bay which has a few disused buildings and I'm informed an old tuna fish canning factory; apparently, they now have a new and much larger complex higher up. The bay was deserted apart from a group of youngsters fishing on the beach. It was peaceful and we were allowed to swim so I dived into the cool water. Clouds were obliterating the sun, but the sea was much calmer where it was hemmed in by two huge cliffs. There were only about six of us who braved the cold water, and it was refreshing, but I didn't stay in too long. The delicious aroma coming from the barbecue was too much for me and when I climbed the ladder in my dripping swimming costume lunch was already being served.

Freshly caught barracuda barbecued in a delicious marinade was being dished out. Papas Arugadas the best potatoes I have ever tasted and a beautiful salad on an enormous platter; it was so attractive it was a shame to spoil it; not forgetting the delicious Mojo Rojo made from mainly chillies, garlic, olive oil and vinegar. Whenever you eat Gomera style you always find a bowl of this exquisite salsa on the table and a basket of fresh bread. We were told to drink as much wine, sangria, or beer as we wanted. It was hard to tell whether I was swaying or the boat but it amused Joe and he laughed when he saw the brandy coming round again.

We left the bay and were on our way to Santiago. The beautiful coloured rock strata fascinated me, and I couldn't help commenting; for millions of years, they have been forming and scientists can accurately put a date to the different layers. There was a red layer in the strata running through all the gigantic cliffs and when the sun shines on them, they take on an incandescent glow. "La Gomera is often called, 'The Island of Cliffs'", I informed Joe trying to get him interested but he was not impressed. He found it monotonous and was completely fed up with looking at the rock face with sheer drops to the ocean. Of course, the boat trip would have been much better if we could have done some sunbathing on the deck.

Today we're waiting for the 5am bus at Casa de la Seda to take us to San Sebastian. It's quiet and still dark and I have a torch to shine so the bus driver knows we're standing here. Waving arms frantically doesn't always work and we don't have bright yellow stripes on our jackets. I do hope it's not one of the miserable bus drivers today as I can't take their objectionable behaviour at this unearthly hour. We can hear the engine droning as the bus slowly climbs the steep road. Further up the valley we hear a cock crowing followed by another and another until they all join in the chorus and the sound is echoing around the valley. It's funny to listen to and brings a smile to my son's face.

The mountain roads are dark once we leave the pretty lights of Valle Gran Rey, and I wouldn't like the responsibility of driving this bus. I sleep most of the way as I'm feeling queasy. It's peculiar how I can enjoy the roughest of sea journeys and yet when I'm on dry land I feel sick; it must be the perpetual circular movement and the hair pin bends. Obviously, the drivers have to go slower in the dark because of all the curves in the road and the journey takes nearly two hours. Streaks of light are appearing in the night sky over the dark ocean and as we start to descend the mountain the first streaks of grey are turning pink.

At the port of San Sebastian melancholia sets in as Joe's visit has come to an end so soon and he looks sad. He may be twenty-four, but he still misses his mum. We cuddle each other with tears in our eyes and lumps in our throats. He waves for the last time and boards the hydrofoil. Soon the Fred Olsen Express is steaming out of the port, and I watch it until it disappears round the harbour wall crying softly as my baby No.1 sails away.

It's chilly and I wrap myself in my pashmina feeling sad, but I look around at my new home and start to feel better. The sun is just coming up and peeps over the high harbour wall reflecting onto the gigantic cliffs opposite; they take on a warm pink iridescent glow. Now the whole cliff is lit up and a luminous red aura reaches out across to the other side of the harbour. It's awesome! Looking up to the higher regions of the island everything takes on a golden hue in the sunlight. In contrast in the distance, I see low grey cloud floating around the top of the black mountains in Hermigua. I walk away from the quay towards the second floor café.

In front of me is the marina as I sit with my steaming café con leche coffee made with condensed milk which I love. I could do with a brandy but it's a bit early, although the locals often start the day with a coffee and cognac; don't want to start bad habits I have enough already. Stretching in front of me are rows of sleeping yachts with masts gently swaying in the breeze and flags fluttering a picture of serenity. One or two smaller boats have already left the harbour and I can see them out on the ocean; I should have thumbed a lift.

Feeling downcast all day after Joe's departure I give up trying to concentrate on my writing. Sitting on the terrace enjoying the peace is a better idea. There's a full moon tonight and it's suspended just above the mountain at the top of the valley. On this island where there is little pollution in the air the moon is definitely brighter. White wispy clouds move quickly in the strong breeze, and you can watch them evaporate. Darker clouds resemble lace as they swiftly race across the face of the moon and bright rays reflecting onto the moisture of the white clouds create an aura of peach and orange.

Two hours have elapsed since I've been sitting here, and the moon has risen higher above the mountain top. Now the night sky is completely clear, and the shining orb looks as bright as a new silver coin. A shooting star gracefully propels itself across the sky and if I had blinked, I would have missed it. I could stay out here all night, but my bed beckons me. It's a shame I can't bring myself to camp out on the terrace. I might have actually tried if Pedro hadn't told me that cockroaches fly.

Chapter Eight

Gone the bright winter sun
and tourist covered sands.
Winter tides hammer beleaguered beaches.
Black clouds gather at the crest
of the valley – eye of heaven eclipsed -
transforming clear morning into twilight.
Elevated palm trees,
fronds yielding to strong winds,
banana trees rustle violently in protest.
Rain lashed balconies;
patio chairs tossed against whitewashed walls
like pieces of litter.
Tops of mountains disappear
girdled by billowing clouds, like smoke;
nature's sounds and deafening silence.
Hard, baked earth
of carefully farmed terraces saturated,
satin wet stone walls glisten.
Horizons have vanished,
no walkers – like rows of ants – to be seen today
on misty mountain ledges.
Storm subsides,
farmers come out to assess the damage
suffused again in liquid light.
The sun's soporific effect on nature
has been washed away as new plants appear,
in obscure cracks in the mountains.

Black clouds are gathering at the crest of the valley and swirling towards our apartments. Never having seen them this low or this dark, it looks eerie, and Pedro says La Gomera is to expect a storm today. It's already hit Tenerife where the airport is closed, and the south of the island is in chaos. Suddenly the rains come, and all the neighbours are out on their terraces; there is a feeling of excitement in the air. Rain is much needed on La Gomera, and my neighbour Paulette says people will be dancing and singing. Torrential rain sweeps down the valley and there is thunder and lightning and a rumbling noise. The much-awaited waterfalls cascade down the canyons on either side of the barrancos and it's a magnificent sight. Soon there are waterfalls all over the mountains and I watch in awe as nature takes its course wishing I had a video camera.

The rumbling sound I heard earlier is now a thunderous roar. A torrent of water comes gushing through the storm water pipe unlike England where storm drains go into the sewers. I Watch it go by our apartments at such speed it is taking part of a wall with it. Everywhere I look there are rivers rushing passed the buildings and the dirt track below is awash. Peter is stranded upstairs in Annabelle's apartment. Rocks are falling onto cars and scooters, and Pedro, Peter and some other neighbours manage to move them to safety. There is a power cut which is not unusual here anyway and of course the storm makes things decidedly worse.

Sadly, the stables look like they could be flooding, and I can see Brenda in a flimsy top and no shoes wading in the mud trying to secure her horses' stable. I want to go and help and start to walk down the steps but one of the local men stops me; he says it is too dangerous. Paulette says the thousands of litres of surge down to the bottom of the valley and out to sea. What a fantastic view I have of everything as it happens but it's a relief to my neighbours when the rain starts to slow down; they were not expecting this much all in one go. In future I will refrain from doing the rain dance before I go to bed.

Time is passing steadily on my little island and feeling relaxed and happy means all the days seemed to be rolled into one. Sometimes I have to check my diary because I forget what day of the week it is. Actually, it's Friday evening and I decide to visit a spiritual centre called Casa Blanca run by a German lady. She started the centre thirteen years ago with a friend. There is a group meditation every night at 7 o'clock, except Sunday, and the atmosphere is harmonious for those who wish to take part. Healing and workshops are on offer and the meditation nights are good but one evening was a little too animated for me; I prefer silent meditating to shouting, singing, and violently waving one's arms about.

In the middle of my friend's spiritual centre is a quadrangle open to the sky with enormous and exotic plants growing and a water feature is soothing to the spirit. There is a large roof terrace and a room where workshops take place. Patio furniture and a large hammock are at your disposal where you can soak up the sun's rays or relax under the night sky. The hammock is my particular favourite and so comfortable, but have you ever tried to get out of one? I can't seem to stop myself from flopping out onto the floor putting my hands down to stop me falling hard onto the concrete; or I manage to turn myself completely upside down and get tied up in knots losing all dignity. Tonight, is no exception so I think I'll stick to the patio chairs in future.

The following day I'm feeling pleased with myself because I actually walked the steep climb home from the spiritual centre last night. It took me fifty minutes but seemed a lot easier than usual; my meditation obviously filled me with energy. Today I'm going to join another group I've wanted to visit for a long time. La Finca is a working farm called Argali (place of light) a commune and a retreat and has many guest rooms; some with small outdoor swimming pools. The workers are called the crew and they live on the farm. There's a good vegetarian restaurant for residents as well as non-residents but you have to book your meal in advance. The vegetables are fresh off the farm and the meals are well cooked.

I'm attending an Osho meditation today. The first one of the day is at six but I'm not that keen. I would have to get up at four thirty in the morning because it takes at least an hour to walk. Meditations, workshops and public Satsangs are held in a beautiful hexagonal building with windows all the way round making it bright and cheery.

There is an air of secrecy about the place to protect the guests, after all it is a retreat, and I'm not made to feel welcome. Most German people like punctuality but I'm an hour early and Hans doesn't know what to do with me. However, I'm going to ignore his 'vibes' and sit under the gargantuan rubber tree listening to the waves while I wait for the four o'clock start.

Later, after my visit to La Finka and waiting for the last bus, I meet Ivan. Instead of the usual large bus a small one has arrived and after politely letting a lady with a baby on first I'm then told the bus is full; I can't believe my luck. All of a sudden, I hear a Welsh accent coming from a man with blonde curls and a huge smile sitting in the front. He immediately catches my eye, and we start to chat as if we are old friends. All this is going on while the driver is putting a pushchair in the luggage compartment. Ivan speaks fluent Spanish and I ask him to ask the driver if he can let me sit on the step by the door. He's not one of the miserable bus drivers thank goodness and he says yes. On the way home the radio is blaring, Ivan is talking Spanish to the driver, English to me, and the atmosphere is certainly livelier than on previous journeys.

My new friend Ivan shouts goodbye as I step off the bus after he invites me to visit him and his girlfriend. They are staying in Vizcaina at the top of Valle Gran Rey in a three-bedroom apartment. There are no coincidences in life, only synchronicity, and I know I was meant to meet Ivan; we feel as if we have known each other for years. Lately I've been sending out thoughts that I want to meet more people on La Gomera and now I'm doing just that; the law of attraction is powerful.

Walking by the sea the next day I hear Ivan calling and trying to attract my attention. He has a similar personality to me, as we're both Aries, and he chats away to everyone. Of course, he has the added advantage of being able to communicate in Spanish, German, some Urdu, and a little Japanese.

Still, I do not meet his girlfriend Lara, but he assures me I will see her on the bus today. She has been sleeping in a bamboo hut on the hippie beach. It's in a small bay just past La Finca called Playa de las Arenas; unfortunately, it's often referred to as pig beach. Valle Gran Rey is the island's most popular area for seekers of an alternative lifestyle. A transient colony is also located close to Playa Santiago. Sensing there is much more to Ivan than can be seen with the physical eye I ask him what he is doing in Valle Gran Rey.

"I'm here to heal myself Geraldine," he answers in his singsong Welsh accent. I look curious so he rolls up his jeans to reveal a leg brace on his lower left calf and ankle. "I broke my back a year ago when I was in the mountains in Mexico with my girlfriend Lara."

"Oh my God I knew there was a lot more to you. I'm amazed you can walk."

"I can now but Geraldine I'm just happy to be alive," he shouts out while looking up to the sky and raising his arms in the air.

I'm intrigued and want to know more but the bus has arrived. Lara climbs on at the next stop and introduces herself. We don't stop talking all the way home and I love her American accent. Ivan reminds me of the invitation to Sunday lunch with my daughter who is arriving on Saturday. It won't be roast beef and Yorkshire pudding but I'm so looking forward to talking to them. We seem to have the same beliefs and positive outlook on life; more importantly we have the same wicked sense of humour.

Saturday proves to be a hot day and I'm glad because my daughter is arriving about four thirty at the port. Peter and I have decided to spend most of the day at San Sebastian. We walk past the port and to our delight we find a small peaceful bay. There is an excellent view of Tenerife and Mount Teide girdled with low thick cloud. We find a walkway and a small tower with a beacon at the top. It looks as though it hasn't been used for many years and is rusty with age.

Finding a rocky area where the tide is coming in fast, I sit on some steps marvelling at the rocks which have formed a bridge. The sea comes rushing in under it at a great speed. Feeling the salty spray on my face and body as the tide splashes against the wall and the steps is a pleasant sensation. It trickles back over the smaller rocks and makes tiny waterfalls and rock pools. Plenty of crabs hang out here and they have obviously found a new habitat by living in the cracks in the stone wall. Looking down I see them peeping out from these cracks and for a long time I sit and watch them going in and out which is comical. Soon I'll have to move otherwise the sea is going to drench me and I don't want to look wet and bedraggled when my daughter arrives.

Market day is colourful and there are many bars open onto the plaza. Stall holders and buskers are trying to make a living. Looking around the market we say hello to a couple of people we recognise from Valle Gran Rey then sit on a bench to eat our lunch. A man dressed as a clown is blowing up balloons and letting them go. About a dozen delighted children are chasing after them. With a mop of blonde curls beneath his bowler hat and a big red nose on that familiar face I realise it is Ivan. Fascinated at the way he plays with the children I sit and watch for a while as they follow him around the market-square; he's obviously enjoying himself. It's incredible to think a year ago he almost died and was in a wheelchair for many months. I want Peter to meet Ivan, so I shout out for a balloon and there's a look of pleasure on his face when he sees me. He walks over to join us where we are sitting under a twisted Tamarisk tree eating our lunch.

Ivan has finished clowning around which seems to come natural to him and Lara has finished making her extremely attractive and colourful hair braids. We walk over to the marina together where there are still a few people selling bric a brac and Ivan gets his guitar out. He begins to sing. I don't think I'll join in because my dancing is far better than my singing as my nephews and niece found out when I was staying with them.

Lara and I sit chatting for ages. She was brought up in Chicago. She is half American half-Mexican and with some Native American Indian blood too. She's an extremely attractive young lady with long black hair and a beautiful smile. She says life was hard because so many people in America were and still are prejudiced. Her Mexican mother used to walk them to school, and they'd have abuse hurled at them and sometimes missiles thrown. Her mum ended up an alcoholic and her dad had affairs which made her mother drink even more. Lara loved her mum very much but sadly she died about three years ago when she slipped on some steps after a drinking binge; Lara was only twenty-four.

Lara's eyes are soulful and have such depth. I sense that although she is young, she is wise beyond her years. It's incredible when you meet people at certain points in your life and you feel you've been together before; it stirs something deep within you and seems to awaken memories on another level of consciousness. Of course, there are certain people you don't particularly want to meet again in this life or the next.

It must have been a hard decision for Lara to decide to stay with Ivan after he broke his back as they had only met four months before in a hostel. He was in hospital for a month in Mexico. Ivan smiles when he recalls the doctors around his bed with their case notes and serious expressions; he would make them laugh despite his desperate condition. One of his strongest memories was when he had an out-of-body experience while he lay in the hospital. It gave him confirmation that it was the physical body lying on the bed broken and paralysed not the 'spirit'. This experience changed his life and made him even more determined to walk again.

Lara and Ivan were staying in Hua in Mexico when the tragic accident happened. It's an Indian town where they all wear native costume, and many hippies and backpackers visit that part of the world. They were in the mountains and Ivan was standing on a forty-five foot ledge built into the mountainside; it was a pitch-black moonless night. He was standing on the side of the ledge arms outstretched playing the fool and howling at the top of his voice. Lara says all of a sudden, he was gone, and she heard thuds as he hit the ground. Terrified she climbed down onto the rocks, but she had no torch and could not see a thing. Eventually she found him lying

79

semi-conscious with blood on his forehead. Realising she had to get help quickly but having no idea which way to go she looked around in desperation. She firmly believes she was guided but she doesn't have to convince me. There was a huge statue of Jesus on the mountain, and she prayed and prayed as hard as she could. Suddenly, she looked at the statue and remembered which way the hand had been facing on their way up, so she continued in the opposite direction. Finding a trail, she carried on, but it was hard going and there were lots of cliffs. She saw lights in the town down below and eventually found an Indian shack which had a blanket hanging as a door. The Indian lady calmed Lara and sent her sons for help.

Lara went back to Ivan with four or five other children who made a fire to keep him warm then some men turned up and two hours later the paramedics. It was extremely bumpy and distressing carrying Ivan down on a stretcher because he was in terrific pain. They then picked up an old truck with a mattress and blankets and it took another hour to the first small Indian hospital. There were no painkillers, so Ivan was screaming all night. The next day they were put into an old ambulance with a young Indian boy who had broken his leg and Lara had to crouch on the floor. It took two more hours to get to yet another hospital, where at last, he was given a shot of morphine. One more ancient ambulance took them to the next hospital which took three hours and they had to pay for it. It was a poor people's hospital four hours from the border of Texas. Fortunately for Ivan there was a surgeon who came every Saturday from America to help the Indians.

He wanted to operate on Ivan but could do nothing without money as the hospital had no resources. The next day in floods of tears Lara telephoned everyone so she could raise the money; he had to be operated on by three o'clock that afternoon. She managed to get half of it, so the operation went ahead. Ivan's brother, Gerald, who was in Mexico with them, was collecting the rest and bringing it on later. The operation was a complete success and saved Ivan's life. The surgeon said he had fragments of bone in his spinal cord and one of his vertebrae was shattered. He had to cut bone from Ivan's rib and put it in where the vertebrae had been, and it took a few hours to fix the metal plate and the many screws. Through her tears Lara thanked the surgeon several times for saving Ivan's life. He said it was his hands being used but it was God working through them.

Lara slept in the grounds of the hospital to be near Ivan. The Indians were extremely poor but made her feel welcome; the women were so beautiful, and their brightly coloured costumes cheered her up. They had never had a European in the hospital before, so it was a novelty. Sharing their food with her came naturally to them and they all took it in turns to cook. Lara bought some provisions, and they were grateful for anything. Nurses were scarce and Lara had to do almost everything for Ivan and Gerald was no help; he had his own problems. There were no pillows and no syringes as all these things had to be bought. Ivan could not even stand a sheet on him he was in so much pain. It took four or five strong men to move him. Lara started to sleep on the floor next to his bed. I can see by the look in her eyes, as she speaks, how hard it must have been for someone so young and sensitive.

"Ger, Ivan was so awful to me sometimes," she recalls, choking back the tears. "I know he was in terrible pain but some days it was just horrible." I stay quiet as it doesn't seem the right time to comment, and I want to hear the rest of her story.

Calling Ivan's parents on the telephone was hard for Lara. Ivan did not want his parents to see him in such a helpless state, but it had to be done. His mum organised his journey back to Wales which cost about ten thousand pounds. Extra first class seats had to be paid for because Ivan could only lay flat on the plane flying from Hua to Mexico City, then to London. A thirteen hour stopover meant Ivan was also flying high on morphine. Transportation had to be arranged at the other end and it was agonising journey.

Both Ivan and Lara cried when they left the Indians, the staff, and the many friends they had made at the hospital for Ivan's long dramatic journey home. Lara said goodbye to Ivan at the airport and the kind ambulance drivers took her back to where she was staying. She suddenly felt very lonely after spending the last month seeing to Ivan's every need and she had a decision to make. Did she love Ivan enough to possibly spend the rest of her life with someone in a wheelchair? Lara decided to join him in Wales.

Ivan was only in a wheelchair for about three months; he could not stand to be helpless, and he knew with the power of his mind he would find the spiritual strength he needed. Slowly he started to move his arms and soon he was able to feed himself and shave. Gradually he began to walk again by pulling himself up with the aid of a walking frame.

His 'spirit' is stronger than ever, and he continues to laugh and live life to the full. Lara and Ivan have their ups and downs because they are both strong characters and free spirits, but with conviction she says she made the right decision to join him in Wales. His family was marvellous but I'm sure being the 'old soul' that Lara is she gave Ivan the love and healing that he needed.

Peter has been wandering around and Ivan has been sitting quietly at the other end of the quay looking out to sea while Lara was relating her moving story. He's now walking back towards us with a big smile on his face.

"Come on Ger and Lara let's have some music," and he took up his guitar once more while Peter and I waited for my daughter's ferry to arrive.

Chapter Nine

Leaving the village of Chipude we call "adios"
to old ladies in traditional black dress;
they wear large straw hats, black scarves
tied under wrinkled necks
and sit against a wall of an old stone house.
Gnarled, work-worn hands wave,
with a flash of toothless grin.

A well-worn trail on Garajonay Mountain,
becomes a billowing carpet of greens.

Fifty yards ahead a shepherd
and his dog, with a herd
of cavorting goats (bells tinkling), descend
the valley in a scene unchanged for centuries.

Ancestral ghosts wander
in the deserted valley. A huntsman calls,
his ancient cry an echo in the mountainside.

Campfires – long since
extinguished – are burning brightly
and crackling once more.
Somewhere on the winding road,
a bus glows in the twilight zone.

Stars wink and full moon casts mysterious shadows
of hanging branches, cacti and scrub;
voices whisper, moan in swaying palm trees,
recall other times. Fingers
of orange creep across the darkening sky,
over the Atlantic. We each struggle
to capture these moments and frame them forever.

Abby arrived yesterday and after such a long journey she was ready for an early night. It's wonderful to see her and I know she misses me terribly; both my son and daughter do. I sometimes drive them mad, and they think

I'm crazy but when I'm not around it's a different story. When you have been mother and father to your children, I think it's even harder to make the break. But I'm sure they prefer to have a contented mum on La Gomera rather than a miserable one in England.

Today, Peter, Abby and I are going to have lunch with Ivan and Lara. It's the first time I've walked to the top of the valley and we're all hot and tired; not too tired to enjoy the contrasting views though. We walk higher and can see the whole of Valle Gran Rey sweeping down to the Atlantic. It must be windy down there today as we can see white horses on the ocean in the distance. It's not much fun on the beach when it's windy as the sand can find its way into such obscure places.

Before walking across a bridge, we see pretty houses with purple bougainvillea climbing the walls and giant poinsettias guarding the front doors; scenery set for an artist's easel. On either side of the bridge there is a dense bamboo forest and thick clumps of palm, lemon and orange trees and the odd papaya standing tall. A natural stream runs under the bridge and although we cannot see it, we can hear the refreshing sound. It's a good time to stop and rest. Springs and waterfalls flow from the higher regions and it's this natural spring water that pours from our taps in the apartment. I do hope people don't pee in our water supply but I'm sure they do when they get desperate. Still the water from our taps tastes like heaven compared to my house in England.

The higher we go the greener it is and the friendlier the people seem as they wave and greet us. Winding our way along the many paths is strenuous but we take our time and as usual I'm thinking of my stomach. I can't wait to see what's for lunch and there's not much I don't eat, unfortunately. My daughter is rather tense coming from England and she also has a few health problems to cope with. She works longs hours and the pace of life living near London is enough to tire anyone. La Gomera will surely do her good.

Abby has already started to unwind. She loves my friends who give us a wonderful welcome when we finally arrive. We have a feast on vegetable curry, a potato and green spicy lentil dish, rice, salad and homemade puris which I watched Lara make. Ivan is a great cook and learnt when he was in the army.

There are about ten of us and we sit comfortably on the floor. My Abby is staying put on her chair at the table as I think she is a bit self-conscious; either that or she thinks we're all bonkers. Eventually, I persuade her to sit with us. Three people are playing their guitars and Julius is playing the didgeridoo. He gives me a couple of lessons but it's hard to play the 'didge', as he calls it. All I produce is a disgusting noise and end up with a red face from all the blowing. I think I'll leave it to Julius he plays brilliantly. and you can feel the sounds vibrating around the room.

During the week Lara and Ivan come to my apartment to have dinner with me, Peter and Abby and we have a great evening. Abby loves Lara and they promise to keep in touch, but the week goes by quickly. It's great having my daughter around and I'm going to miss her when she goes back to England. We have caught up on all the gossip, been to the shops and the beach, eaten in some good restaurants and she has visibly relaxed and enjoyed herself; I know she's received healing from this beautiful island.

Me, Lara, Abby, and Lilly

Once again, I'm saying goodbye on the quay at San Sebastian. We cry and hug and when she appears at the window of the Fred Olsen Express, I wave until she is out of sight. In need of cheering up I go to the market for a coffee as I know the gang will be there later. Sure enough, they soon appear: Ivan dressed as a clown: Lara with her braids: Erin playing the guitar: another friend playing the violin and Julius on the 'didge'. They all ask after Abby then we hug Julius because he is moving on to a different island today. Some of you may think there's a lot of hugging going on, but I discovered years ago a cuddle can make you feel good and it's free.

Erin and I leave the two lovers, Lara, and Ivan, on the beach. We have decided to hitch to the mountains as both of us need trees and greenery around us today, but we don't want to plan anything. I want to go up into the mountains where the sense of freedom is exhilarating. Putting as much space as possible between me and Peter today is imperative because sharing an apartment is not easy and the experience has been enlightening to say the least.

It's not long before three young guys pick us up. When I first told my son I hitch rides he nearly had fit and thought I needed looking after; I assured him it is safe to 'hitch' on La Gomera. The three young men from Tenerife are chatting away and we do our best to communicate with them. Erin is twenty-seven and they must think I'm her mother which I don't mind as I'm old enough to be. The driver is good and neither of us turn green or need a sick bag on the meandering roads. All three of them are talking animatedly about the fiesta tonight in Chipude and the whole island will be having fiestas tomorrow. Immaculate Conception Day and Constitutional Day are two of the most important dates in the calendar; there will be many feasts and much dancing.

I think the lads are saying they're going to take us to a friend's birthday party on their way to the fiesta. Erin confirms it as she understands more Spanish than I do; she's been to Gomera a few times before. We arrive at a pretty place called Las Nieves. The family have the use of a public barbecue where there is a little church and a large play area for the children. Erin and I feel slightly awkward at this surprise invitation but soon we are being welcomed by the family, so we relax and enjoy. They give us meat straight off the barbecue, salad, fresh bread, and my favourite Mojo Rojo; there's also Mojo Verde, which is the same Gomera salsa, but made with fresh coriander. Fortunately, everybody eats it, so you don't have to worry about people passing out when you breathe garlic all over them.

It's a clear day and a spectacular view can be seen of the Garajonay National Park from Las Nieves. The sun is so bright it makes me blink even with my sunglasses on and there's a rich, blue, cloudless sky. We're extremely high up and there is a chill in the air. Lush green vegetation is on all sides and the thick Laurisilva Forest is an amazing sight; valleys and hills roll endlessly in front of me. The ocean is a deep sapphire, the sort of blue you see in travel brochures, and the Fred Olsen Express is steaming towards Tenerife leaving a white trail in the sea. A plane is just taking off in the distance and my stomach turns over when I look at my watch, three thirty, the exact time of my daughter's flight. I swallow hard fighting back tears.

We keep being given red wine and I discreetly pour it into Erin's cup. It's not worth risking a violent headache and I don't want to offend anyone, although my migraines are almost a thing of the past. Many years ago, I found out I was intolerant to orange colouring, grapes, chocolate, and coffee. An Acupuncturist also discovered I had mucous all over my body … and I thought it was fat that was making me the shape I was; he also said I was intolerant to dairy products. I was horrified to think I could no longer eat fresh cream cakes or chunks of cheddar cheese which I adored. He suggested goat's milk which tasted worse than skimmed milk and Feta cheese which smelt like sweaty feet after a week spent in a pair of workman's boots. Talking of which, Erin looks funny in her pretty sun dress with walking boots sticking out at the bottom and she's receiving some peculiar looks.

Soon we're waving goodbye to the partygoers, and we jump back into the car with the young lads who are taking us to Chipude. In England I'd be terrified to hitch a ride. However, people on this island say you can go anywhere in the world, but you always return to La Gomera because it's safe. After saying our farewells and being given an invitation to come back later to the fiesta, we thank the three young men for bringing us so far across the island. We want to walk in the mountains, and this is a good place to start.

As we leave Chipude an old lady sitting against the wall of a small but pretty house, calls adios and waves. She has gnarled and work-worn hands and when she smiles, she shows a flash of a toothless grin; we smile wave back then walk on.

We're delighted with the chequer board of green enveloping us, and we follow a trail down into the ravines. We see a shepherd and his dog walking about fifty yards ahead of us with a herd of cavorting goats. Waiting for them to pass we watch them skipping and jumping; it's a picture unchanged by the passing of the centuries as we listen to their bells tinkling.

An enlivening sun is shining brightly on one side of the valley and in the last few minutes the moon has appeared above the mountain on the other side. We're walking between the two. It's peaceful and there's not a soul to be seen. It feels like an enchanted setting full of wild and magic possibilities. I imagine the burning campfires of the Guanche and I hear the ancient huntsman calling.

Erin wakes me from my reverie when she starts to sing, and I join in the songs I know. My singing is not good, and I sound like the old piano my mother used to have when it needed tuning. Now we are both singing loudly, 'I want to break free' and I feel I have broken free up here in the middle of nowhere. It's a wonderful sensation and you can never recapture the moment, although we all try.

We're on a long and winding road, um that sounds familiar, and the side of the mountain is obliterating the setting sun. Soon it will be getting dark, so we have to stick to the road now. We pass about an hour in silence; sometimes there is no need for words. We feel happy and carefree and it's at moments like these when the child within comes out. We start to play silly games as we walk, like, what do you see when you look at the moon? Erin can see a face, but I'm convinced I can see a face, long hair, and shoulders. No, I don't have a flask of whiskey in my jacket pocket; mind you we could do with a hot toddy at the moment.

We've been walking for three hours, and it's getting cold now that twilight is stealing over the landscape. I pull my pashmina tightly around me. Erin has a jacket with a hood, and she is pulling on leggings over her boots and under her sundress. I think she's making another fashion statement but she's keeping warm and that's all that matters.

Scenery is perfect in the twilight and the orange hue across the ocean in the distance is making everything look mysterious and more beautiful than ever. Palm trees and the many different shrubs are silhouetted against the sky as darkness heads towards us so we're going to hitch again. We're still a long way from Valle Gran Rey and we don't want to freeze out here and be found in the morning huddled together stiff with the cold, because we don't know how to rub two sticks together; I never did join the girl guides.

Lucky it's a clear bright night and there's nearly a full moon to light our way. A few cars ignore our upturned thumbs and drive past but it's their choice after all and sadly their loss. Wouldn't they just love to have a young female hippie, a qualified occupational therapist when she's not travelling, and a middle aged bohemian lady in their car? After about twenty minutes a pleasant Gomera gentleman in a four-wheel drive stops and offers us a lift.

I can't believe how far away from home we are, although we can see the ocean in the distance it doesn't mean much, and we have driven through a few villages. It gives me a chance to practise my limited Spanish on this friendly man and it's a relief to know we'll get home tonight. Erin and I agree we've had a fantastic day and we are glad we didn't plan anything because it's surprising what happens when you don't.

A day in the mountains

The next day the rescue helicopter is out again, and I wonder what's happened this time. It's terribly noisy when it's overhead but instead of flying off it hovers close by. Hearing the whirring of the blades behind our apartment I decide to go and investigate. Some of the neighbours are already standing at the roadside and I can understand a little of what they are saying; a man has fallen down a ravine. My curiosity gets the better of me, so I walk close behind another lady crossing the road. I follow her up several stone steps then past some gardens. My goodness, it's like a menagerie over here with chickens, ducks, goats, and huge dogs chained up behind every house. The tremendous racket the helicopter is making is obviously frightening all the animals and there's a terrible din. The vicious looking dogs are barking loudly, and I'm scared so I glance over once more to check they are all chained up; then I continue to follow the lady in front of me.

My neighbour told me many of the dogs here are kept for hunting and only go out one day a week; the rest of the time they are chained or tied up. It seems alien to us but that is the way of life here for most people. If you complain about the way they treat their animals, they say they look after their families and children better than we do. They think many Europeans treat their pets better than their children and this they cannot understand at all.

The helicopter is just behind the trees, and I can see one of the pilots, oh, I do love a man in uniform. Police and the paramedics are already on the scene, but the pilot is finding it difficult to get low enough, so he takes off once more and circles the area before trying again. All I can see as he lowers his machine into the ravine are the giant blades. It's so dangerous and I think they are remarkable risking their own lives to rescue others. After a long time, a bearded, dishevelled man is rescued and flown to hospital on Tenerife with a broken leg. The paramedics and police appear with his partner who does not look as though she's enjoying all the attention; she's probably suffering from shock. On my way back to the apartment I thank God it was only a broken leg. It could have so easily been another Ivan.

Sunsets on La Gomera can be magnificent, and tonight is one of them. We can't see the sun set from our flat at this time of year, but the sky is orange over the sea and there are some streaks of cloud, in an otherwise clear blue sky. They all take on the same hue, changing from orange to peach to red, dotted up the valley. Over the sea the night sky is spreading out from the horizon and birds are singing in the twilight and taking their last flight; this is my favourite part of the day.

Tonight, there is an Aborigine evening at Puntilla, and it's being held in the garden of a beautiful house called Casa de Lakshmi; Lakshmi is the Goddess of Abundance and I think it's a good name for a house. It's fabulous with terraces upstairs and downstairs and has obviously been decorated by someone with an artistic flair. The garden is natural and has a gigantic rubber tree as its centrepiece. It's amazing to see these trees and I marvel at the height, but I don't think I will ever be happy with a rubber plant in a pot again.

Under this rubber tree there is a large bed with colourful cushions scattered on top and there is a Dutch man sitting on it. He is a martial arts teacher and a masseur, and we wait expectantly as the night draws in. Lanterns hanging on the branches of the tree create an exotic ambience and give a calming effect, as does the sound of the ocean in the background. He starts to play one of the many didgeridoos resting against the bed then tells an Aborigine story; between different stories he plays again. Apparently last week he did the same thing in German, and it was excellent. Tonight, it is good but unfortunately in the translation from German to English something of the story is lost and Peter wants to leave early.

Walking out onto the pavement we see Pedro's truck parked on the opposite side of the road. Lucy is sitting in the passenger's seat obviously waiting for him to return. I cheekily jump up into the driver's seat and sit behind the steering wheel. Peter and Pedro suddenly jump into the back of the truck, and they're both laughing while telling me to drive.

"No, I can't! I've never driven on the right hand side of the road before, and I might go round the roundabout the wrong way."

"You're sitting in the front seat Geraldine, so you drive," Pedro says grinning from ear to ear.

"But all the controls are on the wrong side.",

"No, they're on the right side," Lucy joins in. "Come on it can't be that hard," she says.

"Okay, here goes."

Never having driven a beaten up, twenty-one year old truck with almost no suspension, is bad enough and I have to put my foot down hard on the accelerator before we move away from the curb. Immediately I start to drive on the left side of the road and Lucy loudly reminds me I'm on the wrong side. Once I get going it becomes easier and I go round the roundabout the right way. Driving to the bar Pedro and Lucy have just invited us to is not far but I'm not parking too well. The truck is big, and I'm not used to the width; in fact, I'm taking up nearly two parking spaces, how inconsiderate of me. Thankfully the car parks do not get too full on Sunday evenings on La Gomera. Relieved to be able to climb out, I decide to leave it where it is. That'll teach me!

Chapter Ten

Wherever I choose to live, wherever I roam,
this beautiful planet is where I call home.
The world is my bed and the sky my cover,
the stars light my way, the earth is my mother.

Full of energy today which is more than I can say for
Pedro who has a hangover from last night, I'm walking
to the top of the valley to visit Lara and Ivan at Vizcaina.
They share a lovely apartment with Ivan's brother and
friend, but Lara occasionally sleeps down on the hippie
beach. She has to get away now and again because
having three men in quite close proximity is not always
good for her spirit.

"Too much testosterone up there Ger," she quipped,
when I bumped into her carrying her backpack one
morning.

"Yeah, I know the feeling, Lara."

Once again, it's a beautiful walk which stops me
thinking about my aching leg muscles. All that money I
spent in David Lloyd Leisure Centres did not prepare me
for the steep climbs on La Gomera; it does become easier
though and I don't miss driving yet. In England I drove
everywhere, even to the corner shop and back, hence the
reason for joining a health club. I used to go swimming
at six thirty in the morning, swim for forty five minutes,
relax in the Jacuzzi, go to work, have my breakfast, and
open up the dental surgeries before my colleagues
arrived.

I keep thinking Ivan and Lara's apartment is round the
next bend as it's confusing when the roads are
continuously snaking, and you have to walk back on
yourself. The sun is high, and I've forgotten to bring a

bottle of water. It is a beautiful day even though it's the 11th of December and will soon be Christmas.

Feeling a few emotions surfacing I needed to get away from the apartment for the day not wanting to row with Peter. It's hard enough sharing a small apartment with a friend. We do okay most of the time but there will be a full moon tonight and you usually find this affects people's moods.

I receive a wonderful welcome when I finally make it to the top of three flights of steep stairs huffing and puffing. I need to spend some time with special people and lunch is delicious; it's always good when someone else cooks for you and today it was Lara's turn to cook. After lunch we go outside to enjoy the sun where Ivan and I sit on the grass while he plays the guitar and sings. We are totally relaxed with each other and just do our own thing. Lara has gone for a walk Gerald has gone back to work and Tony is reading.

The waterfall entices me so I wander up to the top of the valley and soon I can hear the soothing sound as I look for a gap in the bamboo; it opens up to a whole new world. Having only flimsy sandals on means I can't clamber over too many boulders which are in the natural stream coming from one of the waterfalls; it's my fault for putting fashion before comfort. I do wear walking sandals sometimes but they're not at all flattering. Oh, the price we pay for vanity. Finding a fairly flat rock next to the stream, with the sound of water all around me, is perfect. I sit in a peaceful position enjoying nature and all her charms. Twenty minutes later I hear Ivan's voice floating through the trees and the strumming of his guitar, so I start to wander back down to the others.

I'm a born communicator and I stop and speak to the locals. It's the only way to get to know the people here and it gives me a chance to practise my Spanish. Regularly I speak to shop assistants, waitresses, neighbours, and the old men sitting on the walls at the side of the road.

Theresa is one of Ivan and Lara's neighbours. She lives further on and has to climb hundreds of steps to get to her home. Theresa is walking to the top of the valley to feed their goats, so Lara and I decide to walk with her. Theresa jabbers away and I listen hard to understand some of what she is saying Lara translates the rest. We sit on a wall as she feeds the goats with palm leaves and stale bread as hard as a brick. It's so sad to see all the goats tied up on the island, although the new-born kids are let free for a short while until they start roaming too far.

Theresa tells us about all the people who have died in her family in the last six years. She is only thirty-eight and although she looks much older, she keeps smiling. Her husband died six years ago from brain cancer, at the age of thirty-four, and their daughter was only eleven years old. Theresa says it's not been easy for her daughter to see her mother so depressed since her husband passed away. She also lost her mother and sister in the last two years and now she looks after her elderly frail father, Manuel. It makes me realise how lucky I am.

We walk back with her and call up to Ivan who grabs his guitar and walks with us to Theresa and Manuel's house; she is so pleased to have visitors. Ivan and Lara have been before, and he often plays his guitar and sings for them. Manuel has a lot of pain in his leg at the moment and cannot walk far but he sits at the table in his blue and white stripy pyjamas and is thrilled to see us. He hugs Ivan and Lara and takes both my hands in his which makes me feel welcome; so much sincerity brings tears to my eyes. I've always been a big softy and would cry buckets at anything remotely sad on the television, much to my son and daughters amusement; likewise, I get emotional when someone shows me a kindness, especially people I've never met before. When I think of how poor they are and what a mundane existence they lead it's humbling.

What a welcome we receive from Theresa. As I said earlier, she suffers from depression and the home could do with a clean-up and although I would like to help, she could so easily be offended. Her daughter is now seventeen and has a baby, so we coo over pictures of her grandchild for a while.

Ivan starts to sing, and we all join in. Manuel still has quite a voice, and he sings a couple of traditional Canarian songs while Ivan is strumming. Lara, Theresa, and I get up and dance to 'La Bamba'. Theresa is dancing despite a bad knee. She is a big lady and has to walk the steep wide steps every day and it was on these steps that she fell and hurt her knee. We all found it hard to climb these steps today and I don't know how she manages; I will try not to complain next time.

It's a hard life and they are poor people. Their house is a four hundred year old stone house and is extremely cold, especially as it's at the top of the valley. Some days there is very low cloud, and they don't get as much sun as we do further down. However, there is plenty of warmth from Theresa and Manuel unmeasured and totally genuine. She moves to the tiny kitchen area where there is a large pot on the gas. Manuel says they are poor, but they always share whatever they have. I'm trying not to eat too much at the moment, but I think it's going to be pointless to refuse Theresa's food.

The parlour is cramped, and we all sit at the round table. Next to it there is an old television and sideboard covered in family photographs. Her daughter is her pride and joy and there are photos of her at various stages of her life. I notice an old framed picture of a man in uniform on the wall and Theresa says it is her father-in-law. He looks austere and it's very much like our Victorian photographs. On the other side of the small window there's a photo of her mother, who was extremely beautiful, and Theresa misses her every day.

Theresa places a large dish of Paella on the table in front of us with three forks. Sweet bread rolls follow fresh from the baker's van which drives up through the valley every day. There's also a local man with a white van who sells freshly caught fish and he is ever popular. You can hear him coming a long time before he reaches you with his music blaring. This is when I turn off my opera as 'Madame Butterfly' doesn't sound that good mixed with salsa music. It is necessary though to give people who live high up in the villages time to walk down to the roadside where he parks especially the elderly.

The Paella is good although I'm not a shellfish lover. It's a friendly custom to eat off the same plate but not very hygienic when you end up with a mussel shell in your mouth. Where are you supposed to put it when your friends are eating off the same plate? I am now hopping around with my hand over my mouth looking for a tissue or an empty plate to put the unwanted shell. Lara and Ivan are looking at me as if I have gone totally gaga and Theresa thinks she has poisoned me. I mumble into my hand that I have a piece of shell in my mouth. Finally, Ivan understands what I'm saying and tells me to put it on the side of the plate we are sharing much to my disgust.

Manuel keeps offering me red wine. I don't want to offend him but I'm sticking to juice. Politely I continue to eat the paella but only taking small bites at a time. I let Ivan eat most of it as he needs the energy to sing. Theresa is now offering us cakes and it's useless to protest; they are going down well after the mussel shell episode.

Ivan plays some more music and then we say our goodbyes. It's getting dark and we want to go back to the apartment to see Tony and Gerald. Theresa gives me a big hug, takes my hand, and says I am her new friend. I don't speak much Spanish yet, but I manage to say, "Feliz Navidad!" (Happy Christmas). Manuel is tired but happy as he says a heartfelt goodbye and makes us promise to return soon. It doesn't take much effort to give a little of your time to others and they gave so much to us.

Chapter Eleven

Atlantic Ocean – yesterday
you whispered transcendental words
on the soothing breeze -
enticing.
White tipped waves, like fingers,
softly stroked rosy cheeks and
gently gathered us up;
we sank into the depths of your soul.

Today, gales thrash you against the rocks,
you foam with fury,
like a rabid dog,
flinging huge boulders like papier mache.
Icy fingers reach windows,
tapping furiously,
your anger roaring in muted ears.

Brigit, a friend of Peter's, is staying for three and a half weeks and we immediately take to each other. I've also met Sadie at last; she lives upstairs in our apartment block, but she's been in England for the last three months. Sadie is a lovely young lady and is about the same age as Lara. Attracting young people is a habit of mine. It must be the mothering instinct in me, or it could be that I have a zest for life unlike some people who seem to have been born old.

The four of us had Christmas dinner together. I cooked and provided the dinner and Brigit, and Sadie bought a couple of luxuries. Before I left England my sister-in-law, Eileen, bought me a pretty pottery Christmas table decoration with napkin rings and although it took up a lot of room it made it more like Christmas on this sub-tropical island. Sadie is a vegetarian, so I cooked a vegetable dish and chicken for Brigit, Peter, and myself. There are no turkeys on the island and Bernard Mathew's turkey roast hasn't reached Valle Gran Rey and only having a hob to cook on meant there were no crispy roast potatoes. My son forgot to send the sage and onion stuffing and the Christmas pudding didn't materialise either, but we still enjoyed our meal. By the time it was washed down with white wine and a few gin and tonics, we didn't care about the lack of Paxo and even the Gomera Christmas cake tasted reasonable.

There is no winter as we know it in The Canaries and this is what attracts people to the islands, especially this time of the year when everyone in Europe is freezing. However, recent storms and gales have lasted about three weeks and I feel sorry for the people on holiday having only overcast skies and not much sun to look forward to. I'm okay I think smugly as I don't have to go back to the cold weather.

Today is Boxing Day, well in England it is, and although it's dull it doesn't look as though it's going to rain so in need of some fresh air I decide to go and find the hippie beach. After walking for an hour, I come across the wreck of a catamaran, just past the harbour on Playa de Argaga. Two men are picking their way through their belongings. Apparently, they've lived happily together on this boat for the last five years and although it was old and rusty it was their home. Now it's smashed against the rocks like a toy and will be destroyed a bit more each day by the treacherous waves. The two friends are trying to salvage their home while their dog, wearing a life-jacket, is sitting on the beach patiently watching. It's sad to see someone's home scattered across the rocks. Pieces of wood from cupboards and furniture are lying fifty yards along the bay; a colander, battered saucepan, soggy mattress, a sink unit, orange plastic seats, a microwave oven door and a rowboat with the front missing are all amongst the wreckage. Looking down from the cliff it's a sorry sight and I can just make out what was the cabin on top of twisted metal.

Sitting on a boulder halfway up the cliff enables me to look at and listen to the waves below. There is something about the continuous sound of the sea crashing against rocks that sends me into a stupor. Thinking of the two men who have just lost their home I contemplate on the fragility of life as I sit statue still for a long time watching the waves foaming around the rocks. Looking up I see a headland jutting out in the distance, a single bird flying past, and apart from the sound of the ocean there is only silence; it's a wonderful experience when time stands still. Stirring myself I realise nearly an hour has passed but it seems like only a few minutes.

Walking on to Playa de la Arenas where some of the hippies live is not as easy as it looks. There is a dirt track but with a lot of clambering over large jagged rocks and the trail seems to come to a sudden end; maybe they don't want too many visitors. There has been a transient community on La Gomera for about thirty years and most of the locals accept it. I've seen a few hippies with glazed expressions on their faces, living in a semi-permanent catatonic state, but the majority of them are lively, friendly, and peaceful.

Arriving at the beach, I'm thankful the tide is out, because when it's in one has to swing on a thick rope to reach dry land and I was hopeless at rope work when I was at school. There are a few footholds in the rocks leading down to the sand and I almost collide with a man brushing his teeth. He is wearing a short T-shirt and his bottom half is completely open to the wind; well, it's nothing I haven't seen before, so I say good morning and walk on. Soon I bump into another man wearing only a short T-shirt and think perhaps it's a uniform? I refrain from having a peep even though it's quite hard to avert one's eyes. I have to suppress a smile while walking past this half naked man.

Recognising a young couple who are fully clothed I ask them if I can take a look inside the bamboo huts and caves. Some of the larger caves look surprisingly comfortable with pretty coloured sarongs and brightly coloured pieces of material hanging in various places; there are candles burning and a few home comforts. In one large cave they have even managed to put up shelves for their CD's and books. Coming out into the sunshine I walk into another naked man with only a small towel around his shoulders. He has a beard and looks remarkably like Jesus, so much so I have to stop myself from staring. Maybe it's the Second Coming? It is Christmas after all.

Lara told me they have plenty of good food to eat on the hippie beach and everyone takes it in turns to shop and cook. The crew at La Finca often send their leftover food along and the hippies have quite a feast which is great because the food would otherwise be thrown away. Saying goodbye to the young couple I start my long walk back as I do not want to outstay my welcome and I'm beginning to feel somewhat overdressed.

It's mid-afternoon and my climb along the cliff, over the rocks, along dirt tracks and across the next beach doesn't take me too long. I'm beginning to flag but soon I'm walking past the pretty harbour beach towards the shops and bars.

Vueltas (Harbour)

Christmas on La Gomera is not until 6th of January. Today is a normal working day which is why everything is open and was yesterday too. I'm in need of refreshment so I stop off at a little bistro near the harbour run by two German guys. They make and serve delicious pancakes with any filling you can possibly imagine savoury or sweet. There are all kinds of exotic fruits and I have to resist the pancakes filled with baileys, ice cream, chocolate, thick cream, and numerous other enticing ingredients. I decide to order plain old lemon and sugar my favourite and much kinder to my beleaguered digestive system; at one time I could cope with fresh cream cakes but not now.

I absolutely love the tea rooms in England where the cakes need serious thought before you attack the mountains of cream and pastry in front of you; where you find polite ladies eating gateaux with a knife and fork. I remember abandoning my fork once and taking a huge bite of my French horn; unfortunately, cream and jam oozed out of the other end and plopped down the front of my brand new Marks and Spencer's shirt. It was so embarrassing when my mother decided to point out the obvious in a loud voice, she was deaf in one ear; I wanted to crawl under the table and hide.

Getting out my pad I start to make copious notes while waiting for my cappuccino. In the bars here you can sit, read, write, and play games until your heart's content and nobody minds. Favourite games in some of the bars are Connect 4 and Jenga and there is a young couple playing on the next table to me. It makes eating lunch relaxed and civilised when you're not rushed and rushed you never are on La Gomera; they don't know the meaning of the word. The food you order can take a long time to come but it's always freshly cooked and it's not long before you fall into this slower pace of life.

Europeans get rather impatient especially in the shops if the shopkeeper is having a long conversation with the person in front of them. It's no good huffing and puffing because you won't get served, until they have given their love to everyone, enquired about every member of the family and said their goodbyes.

Your car could be stuck behind another in the middle of the road because the driver is having a chat with someone; it's no good losing your cool as he'll only move when he's finished his conversation. I often wonder why some tourists are in such a hurry when they're on holiday.

A couple of years ago in England I was having a meal with a few friends and the staff wanted to serve us as quickly as possible. There was no room for prevaricating, and it was like being on a conveyor belt. One thing I detest is a waiter putting the desert menu under my nose when I've barely finished the main-course; he or she is always politely told to go away and come back when I've had a chance to digest my dinner. I don't know if they're on commission but this particular evening my friends and I were asked if we could vacate our table before we had a chance to order our coffees; the next party was waiting to eat. I made a mental note not eat in one of their establishments ever again.

There are still many restaurants in England where you know you will receive a friendly service and eat freshly cooked food. The sort of place where parents still teach their children table manners instead of the fast food establishments where it seems etiquette is completely abandoned. My son and daughter love to relate the story of when I visited Macdonald's for the first time and asked for a knife, fork, and a cruet. It was the first MacDonald's in England and I wanted to find out what it was like. I do wish the Americans would keep some things to themselves. Thankfully, La Gomera has not been invaded by the fast-food giants and hopefully never will be.

Following lunch and a rest I decide to walk the short distance to a tiny beach in the Charco del Conde locality. It's known as baby beach and is a place of natural beauty and interest to tourists and scientist alike. Next to the beach is a conservation area and apparently there are a number of rare species growing there. It's a rocky stretch of coastline a bit further along from the harbour and the small beach is sandy and perfect for children; when the tide goes out it leaves behind a shallow natural pool for them to swim or paddle in. It's also a popular location at sunset if you don't want to sit on the more crowded La Playa. Occasionally I like to be in the silence whilst watching the sun go down. A few restaurants in this area have wonderful views of the sunset from their terraces but you have to get there early if you want to dine alfresco in the busy periods.

Today I've been told someone is drawing pictures in the sand. I'm delighted to say the pictures, or rather sand sculptures, are fantastic and he is such a talented man. Sitting on a bench on the pavement gives me a better view and it's fascinating to see them forming while his hands cleverly mould the sand into all sorts of creations; my favourite is Neptune.

Do I feel like trudging up to Casa de la Seda? No! I've had quite enough exercise for one day. I walk along to Centro de Cutural as I have more chance of getting a lift where the road forks. Taking up hitching was difficult at first because it's something I never thought I would do at the age of forty-eight. Walking here is a delightful occupation because the weather is so good. However, even some of my thinner friends don't always feel like tramping up to where we live. Why not live nearer to the beach and the shops you may ask? Living halfway up the valley means peace and tranquillity and stunning vistas. No contest!

Lorries labour as they make their slow journey up and you can hear the drone of their overworked engines; when I reach halfway, yes, I do walk it sometimes, I begin to labour too. The local council have kindly put a bench under a tree on the side of the road just at the point where my heart is pounding so loud, I think it will come through my chest. Sitting on the strategically placed bench I watch people speeding by with the ease of Olympian walkers.

Visiting other parts of the island armed with pen and note pad is relatively easy but the gua guas, I just love the Gomera word for buses, are not that frequent; hitching seemed the logical thing to do. It took me a long time to deign to stick my upturned thumb in the air. At first, I let Lara and Ivan do it while I lazily sat at the side of the road but when I'm on my own I have no choice and now I don't mind. So here I am just about to climb into a large maroon Shogun for the short ride home; oh, if my son and daughter could see me now!

Chapter Twelve

Lush green valley hugged by mountains as black as coal;
clothed in mighty palm trees, mercifully no buildings higher,
where the scent of citrus fruit hangs in the sultry air.
Papaya plants as tall as pikestaffs.
Banana plantations in abundance.
Verdant terraces stretch the length of this colossal canyon,
like a giant's staircase covered in a thick carpet of vegetation,
billowing in the wind.

Every morning a Hoopoe perches on bowing palm fronds,
dipping its delightfully crested head in hello.
Lizards laze in the heat; darting pink tongues
almost with the speed of light, capturing succulent morsels.
Goats and their kids bleating for their breakfast of stale bread.
A cock crowing, his inner alarm clock slightly out of sync.
Donkeys braying, the noise booming around the valley.
A wedge of electric blue at the bottom, Atlantic Ocean –
glinting crystals.

Distant sound of the waves; music of the spheres.
Winter tides relentless, pummelling and hewing the seaboard.
Swells that can toss a boat like a child's toy or tear you apart against
the rocks.
Valley of stunning beauty, a meditation indeed – until,
an unwanted aroma wafts under my nose, like a pungent
cloud of incense -
grown on next doors terrace and rolled into a joint,
but I'm already riding high on the delights of Mother Nature,
in the Valley of the Great King.

I'm sitting on the terrace, waiting for the sun to rise over
the mountain. It's still warm and I love to eat my
breakfast out here observing this little corner of the
valley come to life. Listening to the cock crowing, the
goats bleating and the donkeys making their racket is a
delightful experience. But I do wonder why the creator

of this universe gave the donkey such a horrendous voice as I sit and listen to it reverberating around the valley.

Men and women are already working on the terraces, but I'm surprised to find so many women working on the land; I thought they had enough to do in their homes. One of the men is collecting palm leaves which have fallen overnight. Slinging them over his shoulder with ease he walks back along the rugged path to the goats shed where there is a stack of them; they will be used for the roof. The strange looking pods hanging from the enormous bunches of bananas are also collected and given to the goats as a delicacy. It's good to know they have some treats. Three kids are frolicking beside their shed just below our apartment. It's funny how most people, I will include Peter in this, go all silly when watching baby animals.

Sunrise has always fascinated me. Many years ago, in England, I remember watching dawn break over Portobello Road and the whole place coming alive before my eyes. In case some of you don't know, Portobello Road is a huge and famous street market at Notting Hill in London. My neighbour and I collected a few pieces of old furniture, bric a brac and a good selection of second-hand clothes and decided to try our luck. I had to try different ways to earn a few extra pounds as my husband was not a good provider. We started out at 3.30 on Saturday mornings after loading the van the night before.

All was quiet and fairly still when we arrived, but it would soon liven up. One minute the streets were deserted the next you would see stallholders emerging from the darkness; like ghosts coming out of the shadows. The fruit and vegetable market was animated by the expertise of men wheeling their heavily laden barrows.

We watched admiringly while they sculptured the highly polished fruit into attractive pyramids.

The baker's light would come on and trays of yesterday's pies and cakes were piled onto a trolley to be thrown away and to make way for the freshly baked batch. One morning we couldn't resist the aromas coming from this shop. Tempted by yesterday's wares we dived in and for the rest of the day had a somewhat calorific feast and it didn't cost us a penny.

We then had to queue up outside the market inspector's office just as dawn was breaking. Everyone who wanted a stall for the day had to take a ticket which was then drawn out of a hat. Most times we were lucky, but on a few occasions, we'd skulk away still with a van load of wares.

By this time Notting Hill was teaming with people and the antiques and jewellery market, which we called the posh end, was pulsating with energy. A treasure trove and most of which we couldn't afford to buy. Lock up shops would open out onto the street and start to display their goods and many cafés were competing for business. Market traders with cold hands embracing steaming polystyrene mugs of coffee would stamp their feet to keep warm. The market was, and I suppose it still is, of gigantic proportion in Portobello Road. Stalls of all shapes and sizes sprawled along the road and turned a corner into the next street the name of which eludes me. This we called 'the half a crown end' where people like us stood freezing our toes off in the hope of earning a reasonable amount.

My friend and I would take it in turns to go and have a look at the other stalls and if we weren't careful, we'd end up spending half of what we earned. I used to love walking around Notting Hill observing the diversity of the people. It certainly was cosmopolitan with hippies punk rockers and some of the ethnic community wearing colourful traditional dress. Some of the punks had such weird hair dos and I wondered how they slept in them. Did they use hairnets? Or did they sit up all night with their hair in a splint to keep it from breaking?

Sitting with all these memories flooding into my mind I hadn't noticed two local ladies beneath my terrace. They were balancing baskets of fruit on their heads trying to attract my attention and shouting up to me in such a friendly manner; I call back to them pleased that they seem to have accepted me. The locals are doing well in Valle Gran Rey, and they have beautiful homes but on some parts of the island houses have been abandoned and terraces lay obsolete. It's so easy to get confused as to who belongs to what family in this valley. Apparently, there are only four or five families in Valle Gran Rey, and they own a sizeable chunk of it. When passing the time of day with someone down at the beach you could be talking to Domingo's third cousin removed or Maria's great nephew; consequently, you have to be careful what you say. I rarely listen to gossip but unfortunately plenty of people do and it's a small island.

Vallerhomoso (valley beautiful) is where Pedro's family originated, and they farm a vast area of land which is why he often gives us fruit and vegetables. Pedro calls down to me from his apartment and juicy oranges, marrows and huge bunches of bananas come down via the rope and plastic bag method. A friend of mine sent me a postcard a few weeks ago but for some obscure reason she addressed it to Vallerhomoso on the other side of La Gomera. After a few weeks it arrived at my apartment, via Pedro, who said it had ended up at his family's house. I only received my friend's card because it's such a small island and there are so many members of the same family dotted around.

It is hard to believe it's New Year's Eve already and it's a hot sunny day. Yesterday, Sadie, Brigit and I went to San Sebastian to visit Lara and Ivan. They're staying on a boat in the marina and looking after it while the owners, their friends, are away for the Christmas holidays. Brigit met Ivan and Lara when they came to my flat for dinner and she really likes them both. She loves seeing Ivan in his clown outfit amusing the children in the plaza which is obviously what he has been doing today. In fact, she has promised to go back to England and buy him a long pair of curly clown's shoes and I can't wait to see Ivan's face when they arrive.

Sans Sebastian Marina

It was a beautiful hot sunny day after the rough weather we've had and we lazed around, chatted, and laughed for two or three hours. Lara and Ivan needed time on their own away from Ivan's brother and his friend; they looked happy and contented. The marina was particularly stunning too but maybe that's because

115

we were on the deck of a boat instead of standing on the edge of the marina looking at it. I'd certainly like to meet someone with a cabin cruiser but knowing my luck it would be a rowing boat he had in tow.

Today, most parts of England are languishing in thick snow, and it is minus twelve degrees; I know where I'd rather be. Brigit is lapping up this gorgeous weather as we sit on the harbour beach. Peter doesn't seem to want to do much, so I've been entertaining Brigit for him which is not at all hard as we get on well and she's good company. Sadie likes Brigit as well but is staying home today because she wants to make sure she has enough time to get ready for the fiesta tonight. Sadie seems to think she needs a few hours to make herself beautiful, but I think a few minutes are all she needs to look glamorous.

The harbour beach is sandy and I'm happily lying full stretch on a towel, creamed, suitably attired, and enjoying my new paperback; there's not a cloud in the sky. An enormous cliff is on the left, the harbour wall is on the right-hand side and there are yachts and a flotilla of small boats and canoes gently rocking in front of me. It's hard to believe the wreck I saw on the next beach only happened a few days ago. We still have the winter tides, and the sea can be tempestuous at this time of year. But the harbour is sheltered which means it's invariably a calm spot and I'm content to stay put for a few hours.

It's a good place to swim but Lucy had to tell me the story of when she first came to live on La Gomera and got stung by a jellyfish while swimming in the harbour. Apparently, there are also a lot of stingrays and manta rays this time of year. Trying to ignore Lucy's voice in my head I slip into the water to cool down and I end up swimming for twenty-five minutes. As always after a good swim I turn on my back and float stretch out my arms and legs trying my hardest to look like a starfish.

Returning to Brigit and my towel I have to hop like a mad thing because the sand is burning my feet. I have tried leaving my swimming sandals at the edge of the sea to avoid having to play hop skip and jump when trying to get back to my things. The first time I did this it was great as I came out of the sea slipped into my sandals and walked casually back to my camp feeling extremely pleased with myself after a long swim. The next time I left my sandals at the water's edge I returned half an hour later to find them being washed out to sea and my sarong was dripping wet. Wading out once more I manage to rescue them which must have made a few people smile but do I care?

Another day I lost my brand new Speedo goggles you know the ones with smart dark lenses, anti-glare, anti-mist, wind screen wipers, the lot, when returning from my swim. I pulled the goggles down around my neck as one does and a huge wave battered me to the ocean bed … well, it was only two feet beneath me. I spluttered, choked, and resurfaced only to realise the wave had ripped the goggles from me. Maybe someone on the coast of South America will find a brand new pair of goggles washed up on the beach; I do hope so.

Watching two pleasure boats load their human cargo makes me wish I was on one of them, but Brigit doesn't like boats. One or two smaller vessels leave the harbour and the odd rowing boat but most of them never seem to move from this cosy tranquil enclosure.

At this time of year, the other beaches in Valle Gran Rey don't have much sand because the winter tides are violent and take most of the sand away. Annabelle says in the spring the sand comes back and the tides are calmer.

117

It's a strange phenomenon and I found it hard to believe until I saw it for myself. I witnessed the beach at La Playa stripped of nearly all its sand within a couple of days. The high waves came in much further than they had done previously pushing the holidaymakers to the top of the beach; they happily lay on the sand between the rocks and palm trees. So here I am basking in the sun on New Year's Eve while my family and friends are freezing in England.

Actually, I do love snow. I'm a romantic at heart and freshly fallen snow invariably inspires me to reach for a pad and pen to craft a poem. Years ago, when I was a kid in England the snow seemed to last longer and was thicker than it is now. We had a local park with steep slopes which were brilliant for tobogganing. My dad made us siblings a terrific sleigh out of an old chair back which curved upwards and had a long wooden seat. Our sleigh was the best as it skimmed past the other children at an extraordinary speed. It threw us off into the snow at the bottom where we lay happily giggling. It was great fun and I remember trudging up the slope with my sister and brothers excitedly dragging the toboggan behind us. When my children were small, I bought them a plastic sleigh which is not as good as the home-made type. I couldn't resist getting on with them and skimming down the slope. No, I'm not in my second childhood I'm still in the first one and I certainly don't want to grow up.

A tall ship has circled just outside the harbour and it's impressive. On Boxing Day there were a few tall ships making their way to San Sebastian but unfortunately, I was slightly hung-over and didn't get to see them. This tall ship with its beautiful sails looks majestic and the whole scene in front of me would make a good painting; I will endeavour to paint with my words. As much as I do not want to leave this sunny, comfortable spot my stomach is rumbling. I wish I could learn to ignore the little man playing kettle drums in my insides.

Tonight, it's the New Year's Eve fiesta at Vueltas, near the harbour. I was of the understanding it was only Saint's days that called for celebrations but on La Gomera any special day will do. We had a brilliant fiesta on our European Christmas Eve at La Playa to keep the tourists happy no doubt as it is the height of the winter season here. People usually go out for a meal before going to the fiesta especially on New Year's Eve and the restaurants around the square have a good view of the proceedings.

It began a tad late and there were plenty of people milling around waiting for the band to start playing and the dancing to commence; nothing happened until one minute to midnight. I don't know whether the DJ was dozing somewhere behind the stage, you know 'manana' and all that, but he turned up just in time. He counted us down with the help of the radio and there was a loud roar as the crowd cheered and the excellent firework display began. Many oohs and aahs followed as we watched the beautiful coloured fountains lighting up the night sky. Afterwards the band appeared out of nowhere; presumably the fireworks had woken them up from their slumber.

There is nothing like salsa to get your feet tapping and I'm off in a world of my own when dancing to this now familiar beat. Brigit is having a jig about despite bad legs and Sadie is backwards and forwards chatting to friends; Peter is enjoying watching the rest of us. There's plenty of drink in the bars and we down a few between us. One of the hippies is fire dancing and she is extremely good at making it look easy as she swings the chains of fire around her body. Everyone is impressed and she carries on for a long time amid claps and cheers. I'm sure if I had a go I'd end up with singed hair and chains wrapped around my ankles; still, you can't be good at everything can you.

A local man keeps staring at me and I'm trying to make out I haven't noticed him but he's on his way over. It's time to dance to the other side of the square. Uh-oh, he's following me and asking me to dance with him, well I suppose a couple of dances won't hurt; Antonio is his name, and he has two left feet. Why can't I find a man who can dance? This one has the rhythm of a drunken sailor. Hey that was my foot you nerd, not said out loud of course I don't know the Spanish for nerd. He keeps grinning at me like a Cheshire cat, so I think I'll give him the slip and go and watch the fire dancing again or failing that I'll go home. I have chosen the later as someone has kindly offered me a lift and my feet are killing me in these high heels; Antonio's dancing didn't help either.

A couple of days after New Year's Eve the four of us hire a car for the day and Sadie insists on driving. She's heading to the Northwest of the island and is driving fast but confidently. I'm not so confident when she drives right up behind the car in front, but I keep quiet as there's nothing worse than a back seat driver. We're on our way to Tazo and finding ourselves on a dirt track is precarious to say the least. Now it resembles the lunar landscape, and I can't help thinking we shouldn't be attempting this poor excuse for a road with a hired car; I hope the tyres are insured. It's worth it though because now we are extremely high up the vista is exceptional and my eyes are witnessing one of nature's most remarkable views. Dense green valleys: deep gorges gouged out by nature over aeons of time: endless cliffs shaped by the weather and beyond them an indigo and turquoise ocean enveloping the two humps of La Palma; it's visible today and is encircled by white cloud. It fills the space before us as it would cover an artist's canvas and I could easily stay here all day. It's one of those rare occasions when there is no need for words, but Sadie wants to drive on. Young people always seem to be in a hurry or is it that when you get older you appreciate nature more and you want to savour the moment?

We drive along a little further and there's a ruine to my right which has wire mesh sticking out of its broken down walls. For some obscure reason it reminds me of the time I had to have metal pins placed in a tooth before the dentist could build the filling around it; not a pleasant memory. This is Rafael Village and there's plenty of donkey power here. The ascents are so steep there can be no other way of carrying belongings up and down. I notice grapevines are growing over the ground of this remote hamlet where they must have some of the best views on the island. But how do they go about doing normal everyday things? Where is their nearest supermacado? How far is it to their local bar I wonder? What if they run out of milk, matches or bread? What if the truck, assuming they have one, breaks down? The mind boggles!

Sadie is now trying to reach Tago near the bottom of the valley and it looks like another world down there and so far away. We come to a sudden halt and no, it's not Sadie's driving we have run out of track. We could have ended up in the gorge and I can assure you the bottom of it is a long way down funnelling to the bottom where it meets the sea. We stop for a while to steady our tattered nerves and looking at the sea calms me. There's a little dot on the ocean, a boat of course, and the fairly strong wind must have changed direction because the sea looks different; it now resembles a perfectly pressed pleated skirt and it's an awesome sight!

Sadie heads off again and finds another track. There's a lot of pumice in this area and it fascinates me to think it could be from an earthquake of millions of years ago. As we round a bend on our descent a wind farm comes into sight standing incongruously on top of the mountain. Wind farms are sorely needed but look strange in a landscape unchanged for centuries. Bumping over a few small boulders brings my attention back as there's obviously been a rock fall. I'm still a little anxious about the rented car but soon forget as we round another bend and the scene changes yet again. Deep green gorges look terrific but I'm praying we stay on this dirt track. We come to another small and pretty village, but it saddens me to look around and see piles of litter. Whenever you come to civilisation on the island you see piles of rubbish and it's such a shame; it's mainly builders' debris because they don't have any regulations in place as we do in Europe.

We've come to the end of another track but at least this time there are reflectors giving Sadie some warning. We pour out of the car to stretch our legs and I want to explore. Finding a pigeon coup in the middle of nowhere I wonder where the owners are? We seem to be on top of the world here, so I walk to the edge and peer over. To my delight sitting snugly down below is a pretty house with a flourishing garden. A fit and healthy family must live here because there are several steep steps down to this attractive property. There is however a four-wheel drive parked up here to make life easier for the inhabitants. Once more I find myself wondering where the nearest supermacado is and I'm amazed at the remoteness of this adorable house.

On my way back to the car I notice a few daisy bushes and red and lilac alpine plants are prolific; there are also a few unusual looking rocks and minerals. Breathing in the clean fresh air is uplifting and the energy in this out of the way place is tangible. Sweeping my eyes around I see satellite dishes, a blot on the landscape, high up on the other side of the valley. It's remarkable how much mankind has progressed technologically but sadly not spiritually.

Sadie drives slowly, finds another track, and further on we pick up a tarmac road. This must be the official road but I'm glad we took the dirt track. The car hasn't suffered apart from a thin covering of dust, and we've seen such remarkable scenery. We can now see the island of El Hierro with one hump unlike La Palma which has two. It was split into two after previous volcanic eruptions and a relatively recent eruption on La Palma was in 1945. It was relayed by Radio Tenerife to the rest of The Canaries and Spain. Another eruption in 1971, which was thought to be small, is estimated to have produced the equivalent of two million lorry loads of lava. It is thought that one of the humps is going to slide into the ocean next time she blows and as I said earlier it will probably cause a tsunami. Speculating which hump is going to fall into the sea, I decide, if you have a hundred-foot tidal wave coming at you it's not really going to matter is it.

Snaking down the road I can see evidence of a recent fiesta. The now familiar bar with Pepsi splashed all over it sitting in the church square and it's another reminder of the modern world; these bars appear dotted around the island for such occasions. We see a few old cars scattered along the roadside as we descend then a signpost for Alojera which Sadie says she is now heading for. A further bend in the road means a different viewpoint and we can see lower down there are numerous terraces. Some abandoned but most of them lush and plentiful with an abundance of bamboo and a few stone houses siting on them. It must have been remote living in these with only your animals in the next room to keep you company.

There used to be a population of 40,000 on La Gomera but now there is only 17,000 and most of them work in the tourist industry. Although some have returned to their homeland there are still a lot of Gomeras who have gone to the other larger Canary Islands or Spain. Plenty of them left for South America many years ago especially Venezuela; it is said there are more Gomeras living in there than on their own island.

We get close to Alojera which is a scattered village leading down to a small but pleasant bay. It's good to get out of the car and I can't resist a walk to the choppy sea where there are one or two fishing boats pitching backwards and forwards. Cars can't reach the bottom of Alojera, so you have to climb down steps and through a couple of alleyways to find the one and only restaurant; of which I'm reliably informed is excellent. From the beach Alojera looks quaint, extremely pleasing to the eye, and has an ambience of its own.

I would certainly have no problem hiding away here but I would definitely need four wheels to get around. I suppose at one time the people who lived on the remote parts of the island hardly ever ventured into the capital and that wasn't so long ago. On this stunning island of cliffs, you often feel like you're in a time warp.

Chapter Thirteen

Past dissolves before our eyes
like a mirage melting in the searing heat.

An arduous journey – to find out if bliss
is the hallmark of the present moment?

It's the 6th of January and Gomera Christmas is here at last. It's quiet in the valley but the atmosphere has been building for many days especially around Los Reyes Church which is looking festive. The winch has been used more times than I've ever seen it used before taking up endless amounts of beer and spirits; plenty of food is also sold in the bars and apparently the large church square will be packed later. Paulette says our apartment block will have the best views of everything as it happens, and she already has a stream of friends arriving bearing gifts. I don't want to watch from the terrace because I'll be amongst the throng. I've never been one to miss out and it is my first Christmas abroad.

Yesterday was Christmas Eve and there was a small procession of the Three Kings. Sweets are thrown to the excited children as the procession makes its way down the valley. Father Christmas is relatively new on the island and it's too commercial. The tradition here is the presents arrive with the Three Kings on their camels on Christmas Eve. We all know the story of the Epiphany, Melchor bringing gold, Gaspar bringing frankincense and Balthezar bringing myrrh. On the 5th of January the parents wrap the presents and the children put water and straw out for the camels. They leave a shoe in a prominent place, much like our stocking, in the house where the Magi will leave the gifts. But if the children haven't been good, they could receive a piece of coal; the presents are unwrapped just after midnight.

Apparently, the bakery is open on Christmas Day so I'm walking down the valley road, and, on my way, I notice a few youngsters riding their gleaming bicycles. Nearing the bakers, I think how admirable it is that it's open today with freshly baked bread and cakes for everyone on Christmas morning. The traditional Gomera Christmas Cake is called Roscon de Reyes (crown), and I want to buy one. Of course, it's busy and I'm in a long queue but when I finally get served the kind lady serving tells me all about the tradition of Gomera Christmas; about the Epiphany which is celebrated all over Spain as well as in The Canaries. The cake also has a coloured paper crown around it and a tiny pottery king hidden inside, I hope my fillings are still strong; it's decorated with glacé fruits which represent jewels. How pretty but I must admit it looks like a decorated bun round; I hope it doesn't taste like one as that will be disappointing. However, it's put inside an attractive box and into a carrier bag. I make my way to the Centro de Cultural (Cultural Centre) where one of the biggest festivals on La Gomera is about to begin.

The Centro de Cultural is a large, modern, and impressive building and it was built with the aid of EU money. I watched a Christmas concert there a few days ago and it was great with young and old taking part. At the end of the show there was a group of teenagers, middle-aged and elderly people playing traditional instruments, chanting, and singing. It's heart-warming to see the elderly pass their knowledge on to the younger members of the community. The principal is an enthusiastic gentleman and a talented pianist. Often, when walking past the Centro de Cultural in the evening you can hear him playing and a few times I've sat on the outside wall listening with admiration.

There is also a small library with a couple of computers where students can study. A section of English books took me by surprise when I first saw it. They once belonged to a Mrs Olivia Stone, a professional travel writer and a formidable lady; she wrote a travel book in 1887 about the Canary Islands. She travelled by donkey for much of her journey in the winter months and early spring of 1884 and it was on donkey-back she wrote her daily notes. The book was titled, 'Tenerife and its Six Satellites' and had lavish illustrations. Her husband was her assistant and took extensive photographs of the islands. Olivia Stone was the first English writer to visit each of the Canary Islands but unfortunately the book is out of print.

Salsa dancing and tai chi are some of the things on offer upstairs and there are different rooms for music lessons. The children and adults I see going in there all seem to have brand new instruments and it's positively pulsating with life and energy.

At the Centro de Cultural the atmosphere is brilliant, and I arrive about 10.30 just as it's about to begin. Luckily the weather is beautiful and there's not a cloud in the sky. I recognise a few people including my neighbour Brenda and her daughters. Peter and Brigit will be along soon, I hope, or they'll miss all the fun. Extremely loud fireworks are going off further up the valley which means the celebrations are about to begin.

An excellent buffet is being uncovered in the square outside the building and is there for everybody. There are pastries filled with goat's cheese and tomatoes, Gofio, which is toasted maize ground and rolled into delicious sweet or savoury balls. It is also used in soups and is common on all the Canary Islands. 'Papas Arrugadas' and the superb 'Mojo' which I've already mentioned are always on the table. There are various cakes and biscuits invariably with palm honey but most of them are too hard for my liking; British cakes and biscuits take a lot of beating. Numerous bottles of wine, water, juice, cola, and lemonade are placed on the tables. What hospitable people they are in Valle Gran Rey.

Sitting on a low wall munching my way through these delicious snacks is not too difficult and I watch three elderly men build a large pyramid of fruit. It grows into a colourful sculpture, an offering to the Virgin Mary, and will be carried in the front of the procession. The statue of the Virgin Mary is left in Los Reyes Church because it's too heavy to be carried all the way from the bottom of the valley; it will be picked up when the procession reaches the church.

A few musicians play while we wait for the dancing to begin. The men are dressed in linen shirts with grey trousers, a long sash, and black waistcoats, but they are not as colourful as the dancers. As one band stops another starts and there is a group singing traditional Canarian songs. A few men are playing guitars but there are some other interesting instruments being played as well. They look like tiny guitars not much bigger than a hand and others resemble banjos. I am told they are lauds and bandores which are used throughout the Canary Islands; they are accompanied by chants and folk songs about ancient legends and romance.

Among these musicians there are only two women, one is elderly, and she is banging a flat drum with a small stick, and another is chanting. An elderly man, who leads the chanting and also plays a drum, is eighty-seven years young and fit for his age. I remember after the Christmas concert my landlord gave us both a lift home. I watched in amazement as this sprightly elderly gentleman climbed swiftly up the stone steps to his house putting me to shame. Living on such a terrain means he has been used to climbing all his life and rising in the early hours of the morning.

Young men and women are lining up and there are television cameras filming. I found out later it was 'Blue Peter' and if I'd known I could have waved and said, "Hello mum." They're getting ready to perform the 'drum dance' or 'tajaraste', an ancestral dance and the oldest in the archipelago. It can last for hours, and the singer is accompanied by the drum with a single stick and the continuous clatter of the chacaras. Chacaras are large castanets usually made from the wood of a mulberry tree, traditional only to La Gomera and El Hierro; the dancers also play the chacaras.

Traditional dancers

They stand in rows opposite each other, and the hopping dance is repeated to the rhythm of the drum. The movement is done on the heel and toe and it's fascinating to watch. The traditions here are similar to those in Northern Spain but it's an amalgamation over the centuries of Gomera, Spanish and South American. I think the chants and music have an African sound, but it all sounds wonderful to me as I love percussion.

Traditional dress on La Gomera is absolutely beautiful. The women wear a cream linen blouse with a lace collar and the sleeve is similar to 'leg o'mutton', finished with frills at the wrist; a black bodice laced up beneath the bust splays at the waist; a long blue skirt with small gold embroidered flowers with tucks to show a white underskirt; red ribbons and a red underskirt edged with black; white tights; cordovan shoes, rather like an ankle boot with a small heel; their heads are covered with a gold scarf and a rimmed hat made from palm leaves which is tied under the chin.

Equally attractive are the men wearing cream linen shirts and black trousers with a red and white stripe on the bottom; a long red sash tied round the waist and a cream linen jacket edged with black braid. On other parts of the island the men wear different colours, but they also wear tanned cordovan shoes and a black hat.

Tension is mounting as the procession is about to begin and the pyramid of fruit is carried on a stand, by some of the local men; they follow the dancers and musicians out of the Centro de Cultural. We follow and the procession becomes wider and longer as we make our way up the steep valley road. Most of the way the dancers are doing the 'drum dance' and as we pass through two villages more locals join in, young and old alike. Any beat gets my feet tapping and the dance is easy to pick up, but I refrain from joining in; I clap my hands to the beat instead. When the road becomes too steep the dancers walk and other musicians start playing; the atmosphere is electrifying. A few minutes later the dancers begin again and move in unison across the road to the path which runs through a sea of bamboo to 'Eta de Los Reyes'. I don't think I'll be getting intoxicated tonight as the paths and steps to the church are rough and steep; they're not really conducive to party shoes.

The colourful procession snakes through the tall bamboo to the steps of the church and still the eighty-seven year-old gentleman is keeping up with the rest of them. There are so many people following and when we reach the church there are more waiting in the square. Two large bars and a stage have been decorated for the fiesta. More loud fireworks go off as the dancers line up in the square and start all over again the now familiar steps; this time they dance into the church and the procession follows. I can't believe the whole group and the people following also enter the church it must have elastic walls.

I make a point of going up to some of the dancers and thanking them and they appreciate this. One of my neighbours shows me his chacaras and lets me have a go but I have to stop my short lesson when the priest begins his sermon. It's a relaxed atmosphere and while the priest can be heard on the loudspeakers the band is getting ready to play and people are chatting and drinking at the bars already. They seem to celebrate anything with a drink on La Gomera. Often, I visit a bar in the morning for a coffee and the men are drinking theirs with a glass of brandy.

Spanish music is catchy, and I soon start to dance as my friends sit around chatting. I'm honoured that some of the locals want to dance with me and they can see I like their music. The band will play for a few hours then another will take over and the whole thing will go on until the early hours of the morning. About six o'clock Sadie, Peter, Brigit, and I go home for a meal and a rest. From our flat the music is extremely loud, and it echoes round the valley. There won't be much sleep tonight as my neighbours will be celebrating on their terraces and when we get back Paulette's home is full of friends.

A couple of drinks later and after a rest and a good meal we change for the fiesta. This is the big one on the island so there will be many people there and they love to dress up. I decide to put on a pair of pretty but flat sandals so I can negotiate the rugged path and steps up to the church.

Antonio, my admirer from New Year's Eve, turns up again; maybe one drink will do no harm, so I say yes to a gin and tonic. He is gabbling on, and I have to say, "no comprender, depechetoir pour favour," (please slow down I don't understand) and I'm not sure if I'm saying yes in the wrong places; I have the feeling I've agreed to something like being his girlfriend. Oh God forbid, what have I done now? Discreetly I walk over to Sadie and start to dance with her while he is talking to the barman. He's watching my every move and soon follows. Dancing with him once then turning to face Sadie again means he is not amused. He says I should be dancing with him all the time, but I just want to enjoy myself and he has no rhythm at all. Why do some men think because they buy you a drink, they own you?

Dancing with some of the locals is great and one of them shows me the Merengue which I pick up straight away. Luckily for me I feel the music and can dance to any rhythm and pick up any beat. All of a sudden, the music stops and it's only 3.30 in the morning. People are saying there's going to be a firework display, but nothing seems to be happening. We are waiting in anticipation and soon the reason for this short interlude is made obvious. Two drunks have fallen down the barranco and are being rescued. Fortunately for them they were so inebriated and relaxed they bounced all the way and haven't sustained any serious injuries.

Oh no, Antonio is making his way over to me and he looks angry he is gabbling on again and waving his arms about and I only catch one or two words like "finito!" It is finished he keeps saying. I stare at him with a bemused look on my face and think to myself I didn't even know it had started. He walks away extremely annoyed just as the music begins again and I'm glad whatever is finished is finito because now he might leave me alone. A valuable lesson has been learned tonight never let a Spanish guy buy you a drink as it gives him delusions of grandeur.

What an eventful day but Sadie wants to go home; it's only 5 am and these youngsters can't take the pace. My son and daughter are used to me and my high energy level. We were at a party in a hall once and most of their friends know what I'm like. I was singing and dancing and one young lady said to my daughter, Abby, "Whatever your mum's on I'd like some of it." She replied, "Water, she's driving, and mum doesn't need a drink to enjoy herself."

Fireworks go off at three o'clock in the afternoon the next day and it all starts again. The locals call up to me to come to the fiesta as they walk along the path to the church, so I follow. I don't know how some of the older ones make it up the ragged and steep steps, but it doesn't seem to put them off. Brigit is staying put after yesterday as her legs are playing up and Peter and Lilly are already over there. The procession following the Virgin Mary is making its way round the church and this happens a few times. The dancers are at the front and dance into the ever-expanding small building. There are not so many people watching today and I'm told the festivities will stop about midnight as everyone will be tired and that might include me. They've put so much time and effort into their Christmas celebrations and I thoroughly appreciate seeing how other cultures celebrate this wonderful time of year.

Musicians

Chapter Fourteen

Dim evening light soothes,
serenity clothes once more
a frail panoply.

Sadie is driving us to Vallerhomoso, a small town of some 3,000 inhabitant. The terrain is different from the south of the island and it's like being on a fairground ride at Brighton Pier. Just when I think I've witnessed unbeatable views I see more endless rolling mountains as the landscape unfurls before me in ever-changing greens and browns. Not so many palm trees on this side but deeper gorges than ever and some with isolated homes at the bottom. Coming into the little town of Vallerhomoso we look back and marvel at how far the road has descended; we have blocked ears to prove it.

We're now in the town square and it looks like toy town with a fountain in the middle of the Plaza de la Constitucion. Stone benches around the outside where I'm sure the locals meet in the cool evenings. The town consists of one small bank, a town hall, a few shops, and a handful of bars; it's a small place but with lots of atmosphere. Looking up from the square one can see mountain on all sides with homes of all shapes and sizes and it is a beautiful sight. Low cloud is beginning to roll down enfolding the land which it has a habit of doing, making it look mysterious.

Food in the tapas bar is great and the people are friendly, but the toilets leave a lot to be desired. I need the ladies but there's nothing as posh as that and I have to walk past the men's toilet where there is a man standing with the door wide open. He seems oblivious to me as I walk past, and I can't help looking at what appears to be a hole in the floor; I give a little shudder which doesn't deter him in the least. Using the ladies loo is an act of sheer desperation after which I have to put my hand into the old rusting cistern to flush the extremely ancient toilet; well at least it's not a mere hole in the floor.

Opposite the tapas bar is a huge monolith called Roque Cano and it looks pretty imposing. Many walkers climb its steep ascent and it's well known on the island, but I prefer just to look at it and even that makes me feel tired. After lunch we take the road to the sea where there is a small bay hemmed in by huge cliffs and a bar at the bottom of the road. There is also an enormous open-air swimming pool which is shut for the winter. It certainly doesn't seem like winter to me, but the locals think it's far too cold to swim. All I can do is imagine myself on a sun bed by the pool with a gin and tonic in one hand and a book in the other.

Turquoise and deep blue sea stretches before us and looks inviting but it's treacherous. There are huge outcrops of rocks, and the waves are smashing against them, hence the need for a swimming pool in this area. After parking the car, we decide to walk by the ocean but there are enormous concrete blocks piled high as a sea defence which fill up half the beach and look ugly. We walk further along a rugged path which looks more interesting, and we can see a ruine on top of the cliff. Here there is a colossal outcrop of rocks which have formed a large archway. We stand under this archway looking down to the sea below where the rocks are large, and the waves are rushing in; it looks incredibly dangerous. There is an enormous cliff on the other side with evidence of a landing stage which was used once by the farming community for the export of their goods from this valley.

Past the archway is another large ruine with mud and bamboo rafters, the death watch beetle has moved in by the looks of it and I suspect there are a few cockroaches watching us from their hideaways; another room is boarded up with bunk beds built into the wall. The sea-view is wonderful from this old building and at one time it must have been a beautiful place to be. Peter and I walk round a stone platform and find a kitchen and there's evidence of someone having lived here recently. Independence and the resistance are scrawled on the walls. Wooden benches and shelves are rotting away; ashes, old bottles, rusty kitchen utensils, rusty sardine tins and an old broom are on the floor; it doesn't feel too good, so we leave.

Caves on this part of the island must have been a smuggler's paradise at one time and Sadie and I feel like we're in a time capsule. The sound of the sea, as always, is hypnotic and it makes you want to jump in between the jagged rocks, but we do not of course. Giant cacti growing on the side of the cliff have huge tendrils hanging down and curling round. They remind me of one of my favourite books when I was young, 'The Day of the Triffids'.

We can't get to the other side although there's evidence of a pathway as it's all broken down. There are no tourists here and it's peaceful and intriguing.

On our way up and out of the valley Sadie has to drive through low cloud and raindrops fall onto the windscreen. It resembles English weather and is a timely reminder that it is winter here. The joy of living on a canary island is that even when it does rain it doesn't last long and the sun soon comes out again. It's wonderful to be able to walk around in T-shirts and shorts in December and January and to sit outside the restaurants with a coffee and a good book basking in the sunshine. It is one of the best climates in the world because it doesn't go higher than 25-30 degrees in the summer and doesn't go much below 20 degrees in January, which is considered the coldest month of the year.

"In these Fortunate Islands, rain is scarce and most of the time mild winds blow; there is fertile soil and there are many crops and fruit without working. The seasons rarely change. The west wind is quiet. Zephyrs carry some regular rain from the sea and cool the islands down with wetness. Thus, even the barbarians believe that the Elysian Fields and the Fortunate mansion described by Homer in his Odes are there." Plutarch

We climb higher and pass lots of beautiful houses with the usual pretty bougainvillea, poinsettia trees and hibiscus growing outside. Looking back, I can see meandering roads with sheer drops to deep gorges on either side. Farmhouses are tucked away and surrounded by mountains; some of them are in such inconspicuous places you wonder if they ever venture out. With hardly any tourists it's extremely quiet as we head back to Valle Gran Rey before it gets dark.

Yet another day of driving for Sadie but she doesn't seem to mind. She wants to show me, Brigit, and Peter the rest of the island and today we're going to the north to Agulo and Hermigua. Agulo is a charming town and is one of the smallest on the island. It's circular in shape and was found in the third decade of the seventeenth century; it looks a bit Arabic as you drive down to it. Agulo is set in a semi-circular hollow with the church dome in the middle and on rainy days the water cascades down the walls. I's a sleepy town and really only the size of a large village so it doesn't take long to walk round this charming place. The church is so beautiful, and the small square is peace and tranquillity itself. A laurel de India tree is in the middle of the square with its knotted and twisted branches and impressive size, making it an ideal spot to stop and rest. The circular route of the streets is easy to follow, and you hardly see a soul as you admire the pretty gardens and terraces and quaint houses. The rugged and dramatic northern coast of La Gomera is bewitching. We walk through the small town to see Mount Teide opposite which is always a fantastic sight.

Agulo Square

Back in the car the scenery changes again as we reach Hermigua, a large farming community similar to Vallerhomoso and the second largest district on the island. At the top of the valley there are the sharecroppers and peasants in the lower part are the large landowners. Terraces were built and cultivated in much earlier centuries right up to the highest ridges. Ships used to load the goods directly from specially made piers one of which we saw at Vallerhomoso yesterday. There are many old photos in the bars depicting life as it was fifty years ago.

On your way down this vast valley there is a minor road which goes to a 'piscina', a natural swimming pool, at the foot of immense cliffs. It's close to the ruins of an old pier which used to receive the banana ships. It's a charming and wild spot but it is well to remember the sun disappears behind the cliffs quite early in the day.

There's not much tourism in Hermigua which makes it all the more enjoyable. A dozen years ago this part of the island was neglected with many abandoned cars scattered along the poor roads. Now the road to Hermigua is clear and much improved making it easier to get around. Many new homes are being built and it's made up of lots of little hamlets. The only disturbance is the occasional erratic young driver and the odd motorbike roaring precariously along the winding roads. As you make your way out of Hermigua the undulating mountains change into perpendicular black cliffs. You only need a cursory glance to realise why there are no houses or ruins to be seen on the surfaces.

Hermigua

140

Sadly, the next day, Brigit had to return to England after having the holiday of a lifetime. She didn't want to leave and hopes to return to La Gomera, health permitting. She's a lovely lady and I'm so glad we gave her a good time and have promised to stay in touch. I know she will always treasure her memories of La Gomera; it's such a unique island.

Enough of travelling in cars, today I'm going to walk to the waterfall near El Guro with Sadie and David, who is a Martial arts teacher and a masseur. It's supposed to be an outstanding place and I've heard so much about it, so a fairly strenuous climb awaits me. I've psyched myself up for this walk and I'm looking forward to it. We have to walk through El Guro first and David's house is about halfway up. Whichever way you enter El Guro there are hundreds of steps, and I mean hundreds. Secretly I'm relieved he only lives halfway because I know I could not climb to the top of the village in one go.

David has an unusual house. His bed is built into the stone wall and is quite high off the floor; maybe to stop cockroaches climbing in with him. He has an enormous terrace with fantastic views of the valley, and I can see my apartment in Casa de la Seda from here. Numerous large plastic bottles filled with water are hanging from strategic places to frighten off the flies he says. Presumably they are terrified when they see their inflated reflections in the water bottle, so they fly off to pester someone else. I don't know whether it works or not but there does seem to be a surprising lack of the vexing creatures.

Many creative people live in this rambling village carved into the side of the mountain and it is certainly different. I am rather surprised, or should I say astonished, to see a house with a palm tree growing out

141

of it. A curious sight indeed, I think to myself, as we walk to the top of El Guro. The last house is a pretty yellow one which belongs to Annabelle's friend Anita. It must be a great place to live if you're prepared for the climb home every time you go out.

House with a palm tree growing out of it.

The first part of the walk is easy. There's a pretty ravine down below and we have to go down before we can climb up to the waterfall and there are plenty of goats and donkeys around. David and Sadie have done this walk numerous times before but if I was on my own, I would follow the blue lines painted on some of the rocks and put there entirely for the walker's benefit.

Scrambling over massive boulders is the only way to find the beginning of the stream; it's fun and after a lot of hard work we finally reach it. We have to use small boulders as steppingstones and hanging onto branches is necessary to cross the stream when we run out of dry land to walk on which is most of the time. It's like being a child again and the three of us pretend we're in the jungle. It does you good to be childlike and we laugh at ourselves when we stop for a rest on a grassy ledge. I'm truly grateful to a large mango tree for shading me but I'm just a little nervous to see we are sharing the ledge with a mountain goat; however, I lie still over-arched by the tree's branches through which I can see peeps of the bluest of skies.

Climbing higher enables us to look back and see astounding scenery. The gorge is narrowing, enveloping us as we get closer to the waterfall, and we can see the valley in the distance; the sky looks like a painted ceiling above us. David says we're nearly there and as I look up the sides of the ravine are almost touching making it look more like a cave which of course it was at one time. We can hear the rushing water now and as we come out of the trees it's marvellous to see the waterfall at last. I have to resist standing under it as it cascades over the stones, so I paddle instead. It's cold but refreshing after an arduous climb. Feeling self-satisfied I refrain from rewarding myself with a drag on David and Sadie's joint. The smell is enough to give me a headache, so I sit a little farther away from them preferring the clean mountain air.

It's always easier on the return journey but David and I have to ask Sadie to slow down; she's always in such a hurry. The vista is superb and although David has seen it many times before he doesn't take it for granted.

I must be getting tired as that's twice my foot has slipped into the water and my trainer and sock are wet. No doubt they will be soaking by the time we get back to El Guro. My calves are aching too, but the village is in sight. It will be getting dark soon and I'm happy to see civilisation once more.

Twilight in El Guro is comical, and I can't wait to hear the frogs' chorus. I don't know if Paul McCartney has ever been here, but something must have inspired him to record that strange song with the same name. I first heard this incredible sound when walking up to Casa de la Seda one evening and I couldn't believe it. There are obviously streams running under El Guro and one comes out at the bottom of the village; it's here at springtime where thousands of 'Jeremy Fishers' gather. The noise is stupendous! A cacophony of croaking frogs, comical for me, but I don't know if I would laugh so much if I had them at the bottom of my garden.

Chapter Fifteen

Thoughts of the past,
fantasies about the future,
are but shadows flickering
across the screen of the mind,
preventing us from enjoying the present.

A few days ago, it was carnival in Valle Gran Rey, and I had been looking forward to it. Men dressed up as women and they all seemed to enjoy the experience. My neighbour Paulette her brother and his three friends all dressed up and the lads looked like they'd done it before. Julian so convincingly looked like a woman and his makeup was perfect; he painted a motif on my face and added some glitter. Paulette and I dressed as African ladies because that was the theme. Paulette looked great and her clothes were brilliant but wearing an African wig with her neck and face blacked wouldn't be politically correct in England, however, on La Gomera it is not a problem. We admire African women considering what most of them have to put up with just to survive.

We met friends in the El Bodegon restaurant for a meal but while we were waiting for a table Julian and Peter went round the bar trying to paint faces. Anything goes in carnival week and most of the tourists didn't seem to mind but some wondered what had hit them when the rest of us walked in. My costume was not as good as Paulette's, and I certainly couldn't put one together with or without a sewing machine. In the needlework class at school, which I detested, I wrote poetry when the teacher wasn't looking. I hated sewing and the teacher didn't like me which she made obvious. It took me about two years to make an apron and whenever I got onto the sewing machine, I would invariably clog up the bobbin.

The nightclub, it is called discoteca here, was packed and lots of people were dressed up including the bar staff; they danced, wiggled, and juggled glasses which reminded me of the film 'Cocktail'. Paulette's friend went home and came back dressed in her pyjamas with two balloons in her bra, a large dummy round her neck and an enormous pair of pink glasses; I think she should have worn a nappy as well. We danced until five in the morning then staggered to Peter's car and of course we all felt the effects the next day.

Sans Sebastian Town

The big carnival is in the capital San Sebastian and that's where I'm going for a couple of days. I'll be staying with Lara at the farmhouse while Ivan is in Wales. Ivan and Lara have been renting the farmhouse for a few weeks and this is my second visit. It's located at the highest point of San Sebastian, and I mean high. I thought I'd climbed enough steps when I walked to the top of El Guro, but I lost count of how many steps I climbed to get to the farmhouse the first time I paid them a visit. The main streets and the square are on flat ground near the harbour, but the rest of the town is steep; the houses, bars and shops rise upwards. Did I say rise upwards? From where I was standing contemplating the climb it looked almost vertical.

Spectacular views of the harbour and the impressive marina with its array of fine yachts come into sight as you climb higher. Reaching the top of the town is no mean feat but it's still a long walk to the farmhouse and I stop several times to rest in the heat. You have to walk past many houses then some large and beautiful villas. Finally, with Lara's instructions in my hand in case I forget the way, I walk past some fields and see the large rambling farmhouse. It has magnificent views of the ocean and Mount Teide and there's a lovely garden in front of the terrace which needs plenty of water. The landlady insists they keep it watered but water is a problem up here and sometimes they run out.

The first time I came to the farmhouse Ivan and Lara had argued so Lara and I sat in the large lounge and did some tai chi and yoga. Although she loves Ivan, and he certainly does her he can be rather controlling and every now and again she needs space. The last year since Ivan's accident has been quite a strain for both of them and Lara often goes camping round the island. She loves to be out in the open under the stars which could be to do with be her Native American Indian genes. She tried to get me to join her at the waterfall near El Guro. I must admit camping out in that enchanting spot beneath such a ceiling and a full moon as well was tempting. Billions of stars in the night sky certainly give you the feeling of immortality and she nearly managed to persuade me,

147

especially when she said she had built a sort of wigwam. However, a couple of weeks ago she came to visit me after camping at the waterfall for a couple of nights with ant bites on her face and I quickly changed my mind.

Lara and I are extremely close, and she knows whenever she is in the Valle Gran Rey area, she is welcome to stay; she lights up the whole room and leaves a beautiful energy in the apartment after she's gone. I like my own space, but Lara has such a gentle energy, and she never encroaches on mine. A long time ago I told her if she ever needs a shower and a bed for a few nights she is always welcome. I leave the windows unlocked so she can climb in when I'm not at home. Burglaries are almost unheard of here and leaving doors and windows open is common practice.

I've made a few friends here, unlike my flatmate Peter, who keeps himself to himself most of the time. We seem to be drifting apart after knowing each other for so many years. I came to Gomera to enjoy my own space and to make my own decisions but unfortunately Peter doesn't seem to understand this. He has derided me in the past but always made a joke of it now he does it relentlessly and it's not funny anymore; the more friends I seem to make the more he feels the need to belittle me. Encouraging Annabelle's daughter to do it as well was the last straw and we had a blazing row. Having suffered from years of disparaging remarks when married I was not going to put up with it again. When someone feels the need to put another human being down it usually means they are insecure but they themselves cannot see it.

Nevertheless, I continue to enjoy the company of Ivan from Wales, Lara from America, two Dutch friends, two friends from England and two Gomeras. Our two friends

148

from England, Terry, and Susan, have a disabled child Ewan and although he is two years old, he is only the weight of a baby. He is a shining light and it's as though he brought us all together; we visit Ewan and admire our friends for their devotion to him. Terry has two adorable sons who are staying with him and Susan for three months and they love their little brother.

It was great to meet Lara at the plaza at San Sebastian then walk over to the marina and sit on the wall watching the fish. Today there are many fish swimming towards the children throwing bread, including shoals of Blue Jack mackerel and Skip-jack Tuna, Yellow Ornate Wrasse are not so abundant but are recognisable with small turquoise stripes. My favourite is the colourful female Parrot Fish which are red with yellow markings the male being a dull grey; they actually have parrot like beaks that scrape the algae from the rocks and it's fascinating.

Lara needs to talk, and she tells me about an incident which happened yesterday and left her feeling distressed. In carnival week the children are allowed to do things they wouldn't normally be allowed to do and yesterday a group of youngsters threw some eggs at Lara. She loves children and is easy going but the incident brought back unpleasant childhood memories. I've mentioned before that she is half-Mexican and when she was a child living in America the family suffered a lot of prejudice. They used to be spat upon and had things thrown at them on their way to school. The Gomera children threw eggs at her as a carnival joke, and they must have wondered why she lost her temper. It certainly brought feelings to the surface which Lara can either deal with or push to the back of her mind once more. There is certainly an abundance of healing energy on La Gomera and it's a great place to find your real self and deal with stuff from the past.

We stay at the marina for a while then have a coffee in the plaza after which we go to the farmhouse to rest and eat before the carnival which starts about 6pm. I put my things in the bedroom which has wooden beams on the ceiling and shutters on the windows. The first time I slept here it was pitch black during the night and a bit disconcerting if you're not used to it. You have to close the shutters to prevent hordes of flies invading your sleeping quarters; there are many animals in this area attracting hundreds of the perishing things. I am not scared of the dark not even if there are a few ghosts wandering around. It's the insects I'm not too keen on although I'm not so frightened these days. I've worked hard on my own phobias the fear of wasps and dogs.

I've already mentioned my fear of dogs and at one time I was so terrified of wasps I'd scream like a lunatic running around with arms flailing when one came close. You can guarantee when you're having a picnic, as our family did many times on the beach or in the country, they will start to appear. As soon as you take a bite on a ham sandwich or dare to open a bottle of orange juice swarms of the horrible stripy monsters are buzzing round. My mum was so embarrassed by my behaviour she hid her face behind her book in disgust and disbelief. Well, I'm not scared anymore since I accidentally walked into a swarm of bees in an orange grove near the waterfall. Imagining myself encased in a bubble filled with white light and where nothing could harm me worked because I wasn't scared even after I realised what I had done; my mum would have been proud of me. But I still don't like the idea of something lurking in the rafters that could fall on me in the middle of the night.

There is a married couple farming the terraces behind the farmhouse and Maria is a lovely lady. Her husband has one arm missing so she has to do most of the work which is tiring and hard; her one daughter doesn't help much. They are poor and the Gomera lady who owns the land, and the farmhouse charges them for the water they use. They can't plant as much as they would like because they can't afford the water so it's a 'catch twenty-two' situation. As I've mentioned before the people on La Gomera are extremely friendly and although Maria doesn't have much today, she has brought a stew; her husband has just killed a goat and it is the custom to share it. There are lots of fresh vegetables in it too and it looks tantalising; we cannot refuse because it would insult her.

Me and Lara off to the carnival.

After our delicious stew and a rest Lara is painting her face and neck in blues and greys and she really does look like a cat. She paints the sun and fiery colours on my face and neck to represent my fire sign. At last, we're ready and I'm glad we're climbing down the steps this time and not up and as we get closer to the town the atmosphere is building. Carnival week in San Sebastian is supposed to be extremely professional and there are plenty of people already lining the route of the procession when we arrive. A few are dressed up with painted faces and some delightful children are dressed as clowns.

The floats are colourful to say the least and everyone seems to be having a good time. A man dressed up as a policeman keeps coming over to people in the crowd to book them and he is a funny character. I can't help feeling though that a few of the themes have been chosen to make fun of the tourists. Not surprising really as some of them do stand out in their bright floral shirts and long shorts especially the ones who wear sandals and socks. Their choice I know but why does a man want to wear socks with his sandals? He ends up with the top half of his legs looking healthy and tanned but his calf and feet with white sock marks rather like a racehorse.

Following the impressive parade all the floats park up around the squares of San Sebastian. Each float has a mound of food and drink and suddenly tables and chairs appear outside each of them. A feast ensues and all the children are running around enjoying their late night. Music is blaring from so many different areas and it's hard not to start dancing in the street. There follows a show on a large stage which is good as a well-known singer has been brought over from Tenerife, but it's the fiesta I like most. Lara doesn't go to many fiestas, but she certainly seems to be enjoying this one. We dance for most of the night then climb the steep steps at five in the morning. Reaching the top, we can still see a few revellers down below but it's time to head back to the farmhouse and a lie in, I hope.

Lara came back to Valle Gran Rey with me this morning as we both wanted to attend Susan's yoga class. Today is

Susan's turn to have the day and evening to herself because looking after their disabled son Ewan is obviously tiring; both Susan and Terry take it in turns to have time out.

The yoga class was just what I needed as now I feel relaxed and refreshed. It's held in a beautiful villa at the top of Valle Gran Rey where they do workshops musical evenings, meditation, and therapies. They have huge green terraces where you can sit and meditate be creative or look at the fantastic views of the valley.

Now the three of us are sauntering down the zigzagging road in the bright sunshine towards my apartment when Lara points to a dog cowering in the bushes; it looks pathetic and is shaking all over. She and Susan stroke the dog; actually, it's a bitch, and inevitably it starts to walk after us as we continue walking to my abode.

"Now look what you've done, it's following us," I groan knowing what the outcome will be."

"It's okay Ger", Lara assures me.

"No, it's not okay. It's going to follow us right back to my apartment and then what?"

"Oh, look at her Gel she's terrified and she looks so hungry," joins in Susan.

"Precisely, now we'll never get rid of her. Look I don't want that dog to follow us."

"Oh Ger, let's give her some food then she can go on her way."

"Like hell she will! Would you go if someone was feeding you and you had no home of your own? If I wanted a dog, I'd have one already, wouldn't I?"

It's too late she is already following us home so the first thing we do is feed her and I, the softy that I am, even put a beautiful fleecy blanket on the terrace for her to sleep on. A few hours later and after we have been fed and watered the three of us sit watching her lying on her new bed.

"Well, I suppose she needs a name what about Star?" I suggest looking up at the sky as night begins to fall.

"No, I hate silly names like that," says Lara.

"Okay what about George then? I quip."

"But it's a bitch," Susan reminds me.

"Well, she's got to have a name so she can be Georgie."

By the time Peter arrives home Georgie is happily ensconced in her new place of residence. He laughs when Susan and Lara go home and leave the dog with me which doesn't raise my spirits. It's Peter's last night. He's

Me and Georgie

going back to England tomorrow after five months on La Gomera and I can't wait to have the apartment to myself again; well almost to myself as I seem to have acquired a stray dog.

Chapter Sixteen

A delicate web
is woven into our lives,
but can be ripped through.

Susan has gone up into the mountains to visit friends and is staying overnight. Susan and Terry take it in turns to have a night off every now and then; tonight, it's Susan's turn and she deserves it. Lara has gone home to San Sebastian as Ivan is due back from Wales and Sadie has come down to say goodbye to Peter. We're in the middle of a conversation when my mobile rings. It's Annabelle ringing from Terry and Susan's apartment to tell us their beautiful son Ewan has died. Naturally Sadie and I are devastated but Peter doesn't say much, and he carries on playing his game of 'patience'. I can't help thinking it's a full moon. Something always seems to happen here when there's a full moon, but not this, not when Susan is out for the night and has her mobile switched off. There's no signal when you're in the higher areas of the island so there's little point in leaving a mobile on.

"Oh my God how is Terry going to get in touch with Susan?" asks Sadie, the full horror of the situation showing on her face.

"You might as well go home Sadie there's nothing we can do tonight, but will you come with me tomorrow to see Terry and the boys?"

"Gel, I won't know what to say or do," she says as she gets up to go.

"Let's sleep on it. See you in the morning Sadie, love you."

"Love you too Gel," she says as we hug each other at the door, and I watch her go up to her apartment. Sadie is a lovely girl and for some reason she looks upon me as her second mum.

It's a warm clear night and the moonlit valley is spellbinding. Standing on the terrace for what seems a long time I listen to Peter continuously slapping the playing cards on the table. He is still playing his game of 'patience' as if nothing untoward has happened. Sending my thoughts out into the ether I desperately hope they reach Susan. Before shutting the door, I look towards the heavens and whisper to Ewan, "God bless you on your new journey little one."

Receiving such terrible news yesterday meant I didn't sleep much during the night. Peter is leaving for the 10 o'clock ferry to Tenerife and we say goodbye at my apartment. I go to hug him, but he doesn't reciprocate, and it was not the right thing to do. Too much has been said and done over the last five months and it's a shame our friendship is under so much strain. We've had some great times over the years, but I cannot feel the same about him anymore. Unfortunately, he tried to control me over the past five months, and I wasn't having any of it. This was a big test for me, and I was determined I was not going to allow another human being to do this to me ever again.

The feeling of sadness is overwhelming, not because Peter is leaving, but for Terry and Susan on the loss of their son Ewan. Shortly after Peter leaves Sadie comes down and we go to their apartment. We are still in shock. Sadie is only young, and she hasn't had to deal with death before so she's worried about how to cope with the situation and what to say to Terry. Having worked in the caring profession for many years, until I had to give up my job, means I've been privileged to have worked with the terminally ill and their carer's; in addition to being a qualified medium and healer so I'm used to these situations. However, when it's someone you know it's different especially a little child, but my beliefs are strong, and I know he is whole once more. When the physical body dies away the etheric body leaves this earth for its transition to the next level of existence. It vibrates at a much faster rate than here in the world of matter. When you learn to attune your mind to the higher vibration you can sense, see, and sometimes hear those who have passed over. I tell Sadie if she doesn't know what to say to Terry just give him a cuddle as he's going to need it.

Although brain damaged at birth Ewan had the most beautiful blue eyes and blonde hair. Terry and Susan were devoted to him especially when the doctors in England didn't think he would live long. He was two and a half years old when his tiny body finally gave up. We knew he had been hovering between the two worlds and he was always surrounded by a pure white light. Susan brought him to La Gomera because the doctors said the sun and the clean air would do him good. He had plenty of sun, massages, and physiotherapy every week and Terry and Susan bought the best organic food they could find; they blended it for him and poured it gently into his tiny mouth. He was only the size of a baby but gave so much to those who came into contact with him. He had immense courage and his spirit radiated out to all of us.

It has been said many times, even by famous people in society, that those born with a disability have done something bad in a previous life. Having worked with people with mild to severe disabilities I have never believed this to be so. It's been a privilege to work with many of these souls and I've learnt much from their parents, who are often shining examples. I'm sure they are born into these bodies so they can teach us. Often, they bring love, light, incredible courage, and determination. Letting them know they are a part of the whole and valuable members of society is imperative. 'Ignorance is the curse of God, knowledge is the wing wherewith we fly to heaven,' wrote Shakespeare and I couldn't agree more.

Ewan started choking and couldn't breathe properly and Terry ran with him in his arms all the way to the Centro de la Salud (the medical centre) which is not far. Fortunately, Annabelle was with him and was able to speak to the doctors in Spanish when Terry didn't understand what was happening. They did everything they could, and they were going to fly Ewan to Tenerife by helicopter, but it was too late. The priest came and Terry, not being a Catholic, explained their beliefs to him, that when the physical body is dead the spirit lives on; the priest accepted it and said he would not interfere with the funeral. The locals were so sincere in their grief as they knew how devoted to Ewan Terry and Susan were.

Later that day Susan, Terry and his two sons arrive at the chapel and we're all relieved to see Susan; we leave them alone with Ewan and they place toys and flowers around him. We are all in casual clothes, shorts, colourful skirts, and sandals. Terry doesn't want us to go home and change; he wants us all to stay together. We're in and out of the chapel at various times and at one point I find myself alone with Patrick, one of Terry's sons.

"Gel, he feels cold," he says as he gently strokes Ewan's face." I don't want him to be cold; I want him to be warm." It breaks my heart to see the look on Patrick's face.

"His spirit is warm darling."

"I saw him last night."

"Did you, Patrick?

"He came to me when I was asleep, and he was smiling."

"I expect he came to say goodbye sweetheart and today we've all come to say goodbye to Ewan and to celebrate his life."

Officials from the town hall are hovering and offering help and support but there is always the inevitable paperwork to be filled out; they are being as sensitive as they can be. Time is passing and finally we have to leave as it's nearly 3.30. We must look a motley crew in our bright colours and bohemian clothes, but Terry and Susan don't want it to be a morbid funeral with everyone in black. It's supposed to be a celebration of life and his was a very short one, but he was such a brave little soul.

Someone has kindly pressed a bouquet of red roses into Susan's hands, and they smell gorgeous. There has been no time to think of such things and Susan manages a smile and a thank you. Terry had telephoned friends earlier who might not have heard about Ewan's passing. David arrives with his didgeridoo and Richard with his guitar so we will have music and singing at the cemetario. Unfortunately, Lara and Ivan are not on the phone, so they won't be with us.

The cemetario is a beautiful place. There are catacombs in vertical rows of four and Ewan's is the second to bottom so we can all see easily as they put his tiny coffin in. The officials stand back and let us carry on and as promised the priest does not come near. We toast Ewan with wine and have incense and candles burning. His brothers have made little things for him and place them in front of the coffin. All of us hug, cry, laugh and sing for about an hour and a half; now it is time for the concrete slab to be placed in the opening of the catacomb and to be cemented over. One kind lady gives us a stick each so we can write something on the wet concrete; when the plaque is later put in front of the concrete slab the writing is preserved.

I've given Terry a copy of the beautiful poem by Henry Scott Holland, 'Death is nothing at all. I have only slipped away into the next room…' and he reads it with a few breaks in his voice. It is an extremely emotional time especially for Susan. She lights more candles and sits on the ground right in front of the catacomb just staring so one by one we drift away and leave them on their own.

It was the best funeral I've ever been to; a celebration of life without a morbid ceremony or any funeral dirges. There was never any thought of sending him back to England, besides the cost, he chose to pass to the next existence while on La Gomera. Mountains and green terraces surround the cemetario; the sun was shining and there was not a cloud in the sky. It was a perfect day.

Chapter Seventeen

Irretrievable past thoughts
melt away
like ice cubes in lukewarm drinks

tomorrows become our yesterdays
the present is all there is.

I have just arrived back from England. My visit was long overdue as I was on La Gomera for about five months before returning. I was homesick and missed my son and daughter terribly after arriving in Valle Gran Rey. But if I'd gone back to England too soon, I might have ended up staying there and it wasn't where I was meant to be. A few members of my family disapproved when I told them I was going to live abroad. They say you can choose your friends but not your family. Well, I believe we do choose our family before coming into this life so I must have chosen to be different from the rest of mine. Years ago, it used to bother me a lot but not anymore as now I am happy to be me. I might be called eccentric but am I bothered?

It was wonderful when I saw my son and daughter at Gatwick airport, and I was looking forward to spending some quality time with them. It's hard for Joe and Abby having to get used to the idea of their mum living abroad. I'm sure my son thinks it's just a passing fancy and I'll be back living in England soon. Sometimes you have to grasp life with both hands follow your inner feelings and not let others persuade you otherwise. When I was young, I always loved the song, 'Catch a Falling Star and put it in your pocket, never let it fade away'; I still love these words and I believe we must follow our dreams wherever possible.

A wonderful welcome was awaiting me when I arrived back in Valle Gran Rey. Susan met me with Georgie dog who looked extremely pleased when I stepped off the bus. Susan and Sadie had put flowers in a vase and the beautiful fragrance of lemon grass essential oil was filling my home; my small apartment looked and smelled wonderful. I was excited at being home and had definitely missed the exceptional scenery on La Gomera.

Left on my own once more I sat on the terrace admiring the new stables on a stretch of ground below the church. I noticed much more had been done while I'd been away. A new dovecote had been erected and I often see these beautiful birds flying around the valley. There is now a new and much larger home for the burrows (donkeys) called Burrow Parque and I'm sure they're much happier because of it.

Twilight is my favourite part of the day and I've been sitting in silence for a long time; going within and being at one with my surroundings refreshes my spirit. Swifts fly past me swooping low between the palm trees. Yellow-breasted Blue Tits, Canaries, Goldfinch, Greenfinch and so many different birds sing their last song of the day. A Hoopoe, a comical looking bird with a long beak, sits in the same palm tree every day. It's a brightly coloured bird with a crown of feathers on its head and it was a joy to see on my return to the valley. Bats fly backwards and forwards as it grows dark, and I think I should have taken my broomstick out of storage.

My close friend Annette and another friend of ours Janice have come for a week's holiday and it's great to see them. They both think I look at home and blend in with my surroundings and they absolutely love Valle Gran Rey. Susan has come over to meet them and has kindly offered to take us in her car to Cherros de Epina, which is not that far from Valley Gran Rey. Susan insists on taking Georgie dog with us and I certainly would not let her sit in my Mercedes if I had one. My space was being eroded once more when Georgie plonked herself back on my terrace; the only reason I let her stay is because of Susan. Georgie followed us home the day Ewan died so I know she means a lot to her, plus the way Georgie looks at me with her big sad eyes doesn't help either.

Cherros de Epina is so peaceful and there is not a soul to be seen. It is bright with spring meadow flowers all the way from the road where Susan parked. We walk along a dirt track and out into a beautiful valley. Tiny cacti grow on the rocks and look like miniature cabbages but much prettier. It's bright in the sunshine with all the yellow and green meadow plants but the grass is yellow too because of the lack of rain. We've found the perfect spot for our picnic amongst a circle of boulders, and it has a wonderful energy. There are beautiful views of Alejera and the ocean below. Annette and Janice have brought a crystal with them from England, and they are placing it under one of the large boulders. Georgie is lying peacefully unaware as we meditate together.

At the beginning of Cherros de Epina is a natural stream with a few water pipes pouring spring water into a trough. Numerous traditions on La Gomera have been kept going mainly because of the island's isolation. Many of them are closely related to water as is this particular tradition; it says in order to obtain the love they desire women should drink from the left to right and from the even pipes and the men from the odd ones. Of course, we all took it in turns to drink from the pipes and

I'm still waiting to see what transpires in the relationship department.

Yesterday, Annette and Janice went on one of the large boats to see the dolphins but didn't see many. Janice was very sick and didn't want to repeat the exercise, so Annette and I are going on a much smaller boat owned by a marine biologist. He handed round a book with every different species of dolphin and the pilot whale, and he was interesting to listen to. Soon the dolphins were swimming with the boat. Lying on the bough with my head hanging over the side to see these clever, playful creatures was fantastic; their black and grey bodies gleaming just under the surface of the water. I can almost touch them and it's magical.

The three of us had a great week and on the last night we became a little tipsy. The taxi we ordered didn't turn up which was not surprising as it was half past ten. We started walking past the banana plantations while telling each other jokes; we reached the junction still giggling. None of us fancied that long uphill climb to my apartment so I suggested we hitch a ride. Of course, I had to assure Annette and Janice it was okay to hitch on La Gomera and to do such a thing was acceptable. We didn't have to wait long as three pleasant young lads picked us up and dropped us off at my apartment. It must have been quite scary for them to have three half-drunk middle-aged women in their car

Chapter Eighteen

Tried to be a vegetarian once, about eight years ago,
It only lasted seven months; I'll never be a pro!
I thought if I was veggie my halo would glow more,
Was under the impression it would at the risk of being a bore.
I am a rather sensitive soul and eating pig makes me sad,
But chopping a carrot takes its toll and I do feel awfully bad.

There is the risk of starvation, which for my body isn't great,
I'll find everlasting salvation, but I'd prefer a steak on my plate.
A vegetarian – I'll never succeed, sizzling bacon is my foe,
Call it hunger or call it greed, but my halo is now a dim glow.
I will always be a carnivore and when I go to heaven above,
Won't go in the veggie door, but the one marked 'pub grub'!

Friends arriving at the port

Three more friends, also ex spiritual students, have
arrived for a holiday and my life seems to be getting
more hectic on what was once my peaceful island. I met
them at the ferry, and they loved the drive across the
mountain to Valle Gran Rey. I saw Helen settled into
Brenda's next door but one and she was certainly

impressed with the wonderful views and said it was perfect. We then took Sally over to El Guro to Susan and Terry's apartment as Susan is in England. It took a lot of energy dragging her heavy case up so many steps and she wasn't best pleased. But she was delighted with her home for the next two weeks. Cathy is staying with me and loves the views of the valley.

The next couple of days proved to be difficult as it's not easy to please all three friends at the same time. Three intelligent, independent women all wanting to do different things is a bit of a strain. Helen wants to take us all on long and strenuous walks. The steeper the ascent the better for her but not for us. Cathy wants to paint, and Sally who has a stressful job just wants to relax. Sally and I are happy on the beach, but Cathy and Helen don't want to sit on the beach at all and I feel like I'm stuck in the middle.

"Right, that's it, I've had enough!" I stop the hired car. "I do wish you three would agree on something I'm doing my best here."

"You're doing a brilliant job Gel", says Sally.

"Maybe but if you're going to enjoy this holiday, you'll have to chill a bit. What if we all do a couple of walks, Helen, Sally and I spend some time on the beach and Cathy does some painting?"

The next day Helen, Sally and I decide to go on a three hour walk. Cathy is going to paint and be at the bottom of Benchijigua Valley in the hired car waiting for us when we cross the finishing line so to speak; are we going to do it in three hours though I wonder? Cathy is not the most patient of people and she'll be waiting in the heat; we decide we'll ring her on her mobile if there is a problem. Oh dear, I think to myself, that's not being positive is it.

It started off as a beautiful walk and not too strenuous much to Helen's disappointment, but we're all in good spirits and we've settled into a steady pace. It's a wonderful valley with breath-taking views which we wouldn't have seen if we weren't walking.

We've had a picnic under the shade of a tall palm tree looking up to Roque Agando, an enormous monolith and it looks striking as it dominates the top of the valley. Walking further along we see pretty houses and quaint cottages dotted about and a charming, secluded house with a large garden. It's the perfect place for someone with an artistic temperament or someone who just wants to be alone. If my kids are reading this, they're now thinking I'm about to hug a few trees, so what's new?

Mountain walk

Twisting paths have brought us to a tiny hamlet with a small chapel and a bar/restaurant. It looks strange to see solar lights and solar panels in this obscure place, but it says in the guidebook it's an experiment and is working well. We need more supplies of water and I want to use the loo as it's preferable to a bush especially a prickly one. I have been elected to find somebody, anybody in fact, in this closed bar. A kindly gentleman shuffles in after hearing me call and is opening up the place for us. Suddenly, the whole family emerge from nowhere and I chatter away to them in my newly learned Spanish. They're inviting us back for the San Juan fiesta on Saturday. It's remarkable how even the tiniest of hamlets have their own fiestas. We told them we would try and come, and they call after us as we continue on our way, "Buenos tardes," (good afternoon).

What lovely people we all agree, and we leave this charming hamlet with its many different shades of colour, hypericum, bougainvillea, broom, canary pines, and palms.

Most of the first part of the walk was on decent paths but now it looks like it's going to be on dirt tracks. There is a myriad of routes between hamlets, and we don't want to get lost. Helen is a serious walker but she's not happy with the map, so we wander into another hamlet where there is a German fellow and a couple of Gomeras; they show us the way. Sally and Helen follow the German chap's pointed finger with their eyes and seem to know where they are going, though I'm not so sure; I can't see a path for looking. That's because it isn't a path it's a goat track but I'm not a goat and my trainers keep rolling on the slippery stones. I must admit I do enjoy clambering down in between the terraces and across the valley and now we seem to be going up again. Well, that is where the man in the hamlet pointed to isn't it? Following the other two dutifully I enjoy the views as we climb higher.

Helen thinks we're in the right place, but we've been going round this same spot now for about twenty minutes. The Locals, who showed us the way, are calling out to us across the valley. Most of what they are saying is lost in the strong breeze. However, I can hear a couple of words, 'arriba', which means up and 'gringo', well we all know what that means. How embarrassing and I'm thoroughly fed up with this constant backwards and forwards. I'm having visions of the helicopter rescue team being called out, so I suggest another way. After all the dried up river bed obviously goes to the bottom of the valley. We give up after only a short distance as the huge boulders are impossible to climb and we must have looked a comical sight. Back we go to the same grassy spot with Helen still moaning about the useless map and retracing our steps yet again. Eureka, we've found it! Not entirely our fault though as the tiny dirt track is somewhat overgrown.

The last part of the walk is quite tricky as a meandering descent makes it much slower and it's hard on the calves. Sally is calling Cathy on her mobile to tell her we will be at least one hour late; she is not amused. There's not much we can do except walk on but at last civilisation is in sight and we can see the quaint village of Targa down below. We still have quite a way to go and Sally and I are footsore and we're all in need of refreshments. There is only so much you can carry in your medium size rucksack. Maybe we should have brought gargantuan rucksacks as the Germans do but I don't think it would do my neck much good. What we all need is a good meal, after a shower of course. That's not easy either because Helen is a vegan, Cathy a vegetarian, Sally and I are hunter gatherers, and I could murder a peppered steak.

A few days have passed and La Gomera is certainly making an impression on them. Yesterday Sally and Helen went on a boat trip while Cathy and I decided to go for a ride in the mountains; just as we were about to leave Georgie dog looked at us with her big soulful eyes. Cathy wanted to take her with us in the hired car even though I didn't think it was a good idea, but sure enough Georgie climbed onto the back seat and off we went.

Cathy wanted to drive, and I kept one eye on Georgie who behaved herself. On the way back, however she was sick all over the back seat. We parked the car near my flat and Cathy took Georgie back and swapped her for a bucket of hot soapy water and a cloth. I was pretty mean to Cathy because I didn't attempt to help her clear the mess up; well, it was her idea to take the dog in the first place. Georgie had only been on short rides with Susan, and it was obviously too much for her. I was angry with Cathy for bringing her and she was angry because I didn't help then I burst out laughing.

"What are you laughing at Gel?" But I couldn't speak for a couple of minutes.

"What's so funny", she asked beginning to smile as I pointed to the driver's seat where there was a large dead and stiff lizard. Cathy must have been sitting on it all the way back from La Laguna Grande, a beautiful spot, where we had stopped and sat near the trees. There's a legend that on the night of the full moon at La Laguna Grande all the witches of the island dance naked and make agreements with the devil. Well, I didn't see any witches but I'm now looking at this dead lizard which we seemed to have brought back as a souvenir.

"You've squashed the poor thing," I said and now we were both laughing. "Hell, we're going to be late picking the girls up from the harbour," I said suddenly noticing the clock on the dashboard.

"Oh heck, I'll just run this bucket back to your flat."

"Okay!"

Looking at the poor lizard I started laughing again and when Cathy returned, she gently moved it to the side of the road and climbed into the car. She drove like a mad thing and when we arrived the boat was in but there was no sign of Helen and Sally. We waited for half an hour and made our way back to my apartment rather puzzled. I'd been trying to get hold of them on the mobile to no avail; the reception is often bad here because of the topography of the island.

Sally and Helen arrived home a short while after us, looking tired and utterly fed up because they had disembarked at the wrong harbour. Sally was feeling so sick, and they didn't notice they were at Santiago instead of Vueltas until the boat was out of sight. They had tried to ring my mobile, but they couldn't get through either and it cost them a small fortune to get back to Valle Gran Rey by taxi.

It didn't cheer them up much when Cathy told them about Georgie being sick on the back seat of the car. In fact, they were extremely annoyed because they'll have to sit on damp seats tomorrow. Things were getting a bit fraught, so I made them laugh when I told them about the poor unfortunate lizard. They found it highly amusing and the two of them bought a rubber lizard the next day. It looked real and it was the same colour as the one that had been squashed. When they were on the plane going home and Cathy went to the loo, they placed it on her seat. They all had a good giggle and Cathy took it in good part.

Chapter Nineteen

La Gomera's fiestas have started,
You'll be dancing through the night.
Sashay your hips to the beat now,
Dance salsa with all your might.
Salsa is dancing with rhythm,
Like you've never danced before.
Sashay your hips to the beat now,
Move your feet across the floor.

Moving with a partner is better,
As long as you know him well,
Sashaying your hips to the beat,
His passions you'll have to quell.
You won't want to stop swaying,
Moving and grooving for sure.
Sashay your hips to the beat now,
Move your feet across the floor.

On black sanded beaches you'll rest,
A well-earned break – you take five.
Sashay your hips to the beat now,
While the plaza comes alive.
Bands from Tenerife have played,
Like they've never played before.
Sashay your hips to the beat now,
Move your feet across the floor.

Don't worry about your bedtime,
Dance until the early morning.
Sashay your hips to the beat now,
But there is one word of warning.
Your body will certainly ache,
Like it's never ached before.
Sashay your hips to the beat now,
Move your feet across the floor.

San Juan Fiesta is 26th of June and is held in the same
church as Los Reyes, so the three kings and Saint John

share the same church. I asked one of the local women if I could go into the church and have a look as I was in the courtyard reading; she was tidying it up before the fiesta. Sitting in the pew enjoying the silence I looked up and saw the lady with her hands up Madonna's dress obviously she was changing her clothes, but I had to stop myself from grinning.

I met Manuel at the San Juan fiesta and we danced well together like a couple of pros in fact and it's brilliant to find a man who can actually dance properly. We said we'd meet a few days later at the San Pedro fiesta, whose little chapel is down at La Playa. There is a procession of boats which starts early evening so I'm walking down with plenty of time to spare. Mind you, Gomera time is not like English time, and nothing ever starts when it's supposed to. As I walk past the many souvenir stalls, bars, and food vans, I can feel the atmosphere building.

There's a procession of boats waiting; boats of many different shapes, sizes, and colours. It leaves from the beach and makes its way to the harbour and back again. If you want to get in one of them you have to scramble, but I'm not bothering as I don't recognise anyone. One of the boats inevitably has fireworks on it which are set off every few minutes and of course the statue of San Pedro has a small boat to himself. There is much drinking, dancing, and singing on the boats which looks precarious to say the least but I'm sure if anyone falls in, they'll get fished out immediately.

An hour and a half later when all the boats have returned and divested themselves of most of the revellers the religious service begins outside the little chapel in the square. Flowers inside the chapel, arranged by my German friend who runs the spiritual centre are absolutely beautiful and the square is packed. Traditional dancing, chanting, and singing follows much to my delight and I'm enthralled once again when I watch the drum dance and listen to the percussion instruments. The continuous rhythm of this ancestral dance and clattering of the chacaras is absorbing and I don't want it to stop. But it is time for everyone to eat before the partying begins in earnest.

Manuel arrives and after a couple of drinks we dance. We end up dancing all night until six-thirty in the morning; with a few rest breaks on the beach. He's not too pleased about me hitching a lift home as there are a lot of youngsters from Tenerife here. I said goodbye to him but could not believe my luck when I climbed into a van and realised it was Antonio. He is Jabbering on and he and wants to know why I like Manuel and not him; he must have been spying on me all night. Arriving at my apartment a few minutes later he tries to grab my arm, so I jump out pretty swiftly and slam the door on him. It was the first time I'd had any trouble hitching but that seems to be Antonio's style. I'm definitely going to keep well away from him in future.

Manuel informed me there was going to be a free lunch for everyone the next day and asked me to meet him at La Playa. Sure enough, there is a colossal paella being served with fresh bread. I'm amazed at the size of it but there are a lot of people to feed. The locals are polite and friendly and are making sure everyone is full and happy.

There are all sorts of rides and side shows for the children and Manuel has already told me about the espooma (foam) on the beach which it sounds like fun. A rather large gentleman has an enormous gun and espooma is shooting out of it at great speed. It's supposed to be for the kids but there are many adults dancing in the foam. More is showered over the large crowd and the sand becomes wet and soggy, but no one seems to mind.

My friend Vicky has arrived for a week's holiday and I'm glad she chose July as this week is the Del Carmen fiesta. It's one of the biggest on the islands and in Spain and it lasts for five days. Vicky loves la Gomera especially Valle Gran Rey and she thinks it's one of the most beautiful valleys she ever seen; most people say the same. She also thinks Georgie dog is beautiful. Everyone loves Georgie but no one wants to take her off my hands. I'll never get rid of my stray dog while all these people keep cooing over her. I can just about afford the rent and food for myself let alone feed a dog as well.

Vicky is looking forward to the fiesta but her and Susan will be along later to join Sadie and myself. The procession of boats is much bigger than the one at the San Pedro fiesta and we go down to the harbour in the hope we'll be allowed on board one of them. My neighbour Brenda will be there, and she said we can get on one of the larger boats with her.

They mean business here. All the boats are decorated, small medium or large, with an abundance of blue, pink, and white bunting. We follow Brenda and her two daughters but it's a bit of a scramble as everyone has the same idea; all except Manuel that is, he doesn't like boats and he is content to watch from dry land.

It's wonderful to see the way the Gomeras enjoy their fiestas and I've never seen so many boats in one procession. There are a lot of smaller vessels in between the bigger ones and right in the middle is a boat carrying a statue of Del Carmen. This is followed by another smaller boat with the all-important fireworks on board. Everyone is entering into the fun and there are many cans of beer being loaded onto the boats. One of them is packed full of youngsters and they're dancing and singing, and I don't know how they haven't fallen overboard. Anyway, we're now on the 'Tina' owned by a friend of Brenda's which it's pretty comfortable and we have a wonderful view of everything. It's a while before the procession gets going, but eventually we start to move away from the harbour. The noise is stupendous with the loudest fireworks you can imagine plus hooters going off and people singing. After about an hour, the whole flotilla of boats stops at a large, pretty bay and some decide to dive into the sea fully clothed. Lots of people wave to us from the beach and more fireworks go off. It's a carnival atmosphere and now we're on our way back to the harbour; about two and a half hours have past and it's been brilliant.

Vicky and I have decided to go to some of the events being staged for the fiesta. The harbour is throbbing with activity and there are so many stalls, bars and eating places to choose from. Hordes of people are sitting along the top of the harbour wall eagerly waiting for the fun to begin but it doesn't look too promising. A greased goat is being let loose and the men have to try to catch it without being butted. To me and Vicky it's silly and cruel but obviously a great sport to the locals and an age-old tradition. There is much raucous laughter coming from the men who seem to be enjoying themselves and the audience is enraptured but we decide to move away.

Vicky has gone back to my flat for a rest and Sadie has joined me and Manuel. The bars seem to be open all day and we decide to go to a good fish restaurant which proves to be a great meal. Sadie and I have to speak Spanish all the time because Manuel does not speak English but it's great practise; my Spanish is improving every day. Afterwards we go back to the fiesta as the music and dancing is now under way again. Manuel and I dance most of the night and Sadie is surprised at how well we dance together and how fast we whirl round the square.

The salsa bands are quite good but a short while back I saw a fantastic Cuban band called the 'Fakires'. They were touring Tenerife and popped over to do a concert near the harbour. Most of them were in their seventies but were extremely fit and the lead singer was a brilliant dancer. They play bongos and other percussion instruments, saxophone, maracas and tres guitar. Salsa originated from Cuba and is not the same as the Spanish version. The 'Fakires' was the real thing with captivating sounds and intoxicating rhythms. I've since found out it is called rural Cuban music. Listening with your eyes shut was like being transported to Cuba and I wish the concert had lasted for more than an hour; it's such happy music.

It was all great fun but I'm glad the fiestas have finished for a while. Casa de la Seda and my apartment are peaceful and it's good for Vicky to relax before she goes back to England. She's has a lot of stress to cope with so a week's holiday is not enough and by the time she winds down it will be time for her to go home. She loves the views from my apartment in the day and at night she is mesmerised when we sit on my terrace looking at the fabulous night sky; she can't remember the last time she saw such a fantastic sight.

Vicky wants to take Georgie dog home with her to England and my face lights up, but I know it's impossible. There are so many stray dogs on the island, and nothing is done about them. I had a terrible time when Susan was in England, and I found out Georgie was 'on heat'. After a few exhausting nights of throwing water over the dogs that were making their way up the steps and finally barricading Georgie in she still became pregnant. One stray dog was more than enough but puppies, Oh God! Besides that, I'm fed up with Georgie following me everywhere and I cannot move without her close on my heels. She pursues me all the way down to La Playa and even tries to follow me into the shops, bars, and restaurants, where she gets shooed out time after time. Realising I'm probably the first person to show her any affection means she's bound to tag along beside me but I'm beginning to feel I'm stuck with her. It was Lara and Susan who brought Georgie back to my apartment, but Lara is off camping around the island, Susan is liable to go off travelling at any moment and I will have to go back to England for a few weeks to sort out my house. It's not possible for either of them to have a stray dog and I feel trapped; think I'm being taught another lesson on how not to let others force me into a corner.

A couple of weeks have gone by since Vicky went home and there has been another fiesta at Arure this time. It's a village further up the mountain not far from Valle Gran Rey. Arure is famous for its bees and their honey which is pure and scented. Old houses in this village are splendid examples of Canarian architecture and from Arure there are some lovely and not too strenuous walks. There is also a marvellous viewpoint, Mirador Ermita El Santo, down a dirt track and under a small bridge. Stunning views of Taguluche can be seen from here and also the island of La Palma on a clear day.

A fiesta at the gorgeous hamlet Los Asevinos is being held next. It's near El Cedro which you get to through the heart of the rain forest. This part of the island is particularly stunning and different again. The forest is a wonderful place to walk and it's not difficult to imagine yourself lost in time once more. I did the walk with friends and was so glad of the experience. Putting my hiking boots on was wise as some of the time we were walking on, or should I say sliding on, slippery roots or jumping across rushing streams.

We were silent for most of the trek which allowed us to hear the beautiful birdsong, the insects, and the sound of running water. With so many remarkable sights, colours, and aromas in this mysterious rain forest I thought I had passed from the physical body and entered the heavenly realms. I soon realised I was still on earth when I tripped over a thick tree root hidden by wet slippery leaves and ended up sprawled on the damp ground. A large bottle of water from my rucksack nearly knocked me out, well, it would have done if it had still been full.

We stopped to view a tiny chapel, the Ermitage of Nuestra Senora de Lourdes, ermitage meaning place of homage, and it has a tiny altar and wooden benches. It's the focus for an annual pilgrimage through the dark forest on the last Sunday in August. After a quick look we carried on past the little chapel for the last part of the trail. We walked for about three hours and towards the end when the trees were not so thick the heat intensified; we knew we were coming to the edge of the forest. However, we soon forgot the heat when we entered the hamlet of El Cedro. Houses looked like they were grafted onto the banks of this fabulous gorge so steep were they. A blue, cloudless sky made me blink a few times and the sea filling the triangle at the bottom of the valley was dazzling in the brilliant sunshine.

Los Asevinos is tiny and an extremely quiet hamlet which doesn't even have a bar except when a fiesta is being held. Now it is inundated with people from all over the island and of course some of the locals from my valley are here too. I'm looking forward to the music and dancing. There are bars and food caravans set up in numerous places and I have never tasted pork like it. It's served with papas arugadas, fresh bread and mojo; the pork is cooked in spices is absolutely delicious and melts in the mouth. Much against my strict English upbringing I even mop the sauce up with my bread as is the custom here; I feel like a naughty child.

The rain forest.

Chapter Twenty

Floating on my back
looking up at black mountains
vast ocean calms me
puts things into perspective
on this volcanic island.

It is my first summer in The Canaries and thirty degrees is sufficiently hot for me. If you don't take a siesta in April, you certainly do in August. The Atlantic is nearly always cold but it's a welcome relief to slide into the cool water when you've been sunbathing. Three hours on the beach is enough, once, or twice a week and I love to read a book while lying full stretch on the sand. Manuel doesn't come to the beach much as he works long hours most days, but we do have some wonderful weekends together; when he hires a car and I drive us to different parts of the island. He's extremely romantic but there's a warning bell ringing in my head. Spanish men are romantic and it's flattering at the time and of course the poet in me loves romance. Men actually mean what they are saying when they are saying it, but it doesn't always stand the test of time.

In the meantime, Georgie dog had two puppies under a rock on the terrace below my apartment, but the third puppy was too large, and she was walking around with it still inside her. Fortunately, Susan and I realised something was wrong. Between me, Susan, Chloe and with Brenda on the telephone trying to tell us what to do. We tried desperately to pull out the last puppy, to no avail. Later in the day I had to half carry her up two flights of stairs and suffering from cervical spondylosis meant I was in agony for the next three days and had to lie flat. Susan was expecting a baby so there was no way she could carry a heavy dog. Halfway to the vets the puppy slithered out onto the blanket Susan had put on the back seat of her car. After a couple of visits and a vet's bill later Georgie was on the mend. We shared the vet's bill and bought some capsules to get rid of the fleas. By now I'd certainly had enough of stray dogs and my purse was empty once more. Eventually Pedro found a home for Georgie on the other side of the island when Susan and I were in England so there was a happy ending.

Life has changed here or should I say Pedro has changed since his partner Lucy went back to Germany for good. He threw Annabelle out of her apartment a couple of months ago and we don't know why? Her and Lucy were friends but since Lucy left Pedro has been understandably grumpy. He's been smoking the 'wacky backy' more than ever if that's possible. The pungent aroma wafts permanently from his apartment and Paulette also smokes it so the smell often drifts over from next door as well; it's a wonder I don't get high just living in this apartment block.

What happened between Pedro and Lucy, I do not know, but he seemed to take it out on Annabelle. I don't feel secure anymore and I asked Paulette if she thought Pedro would throw us out too, as she knows him better than I do. She said she didn't know what had happened between Annabelle and Pedro, but it was nothing to do with us. In England I was having a lot of worry with my house, and I had to go back to sort things out. Mistakenly I suppressed my uneasiness about Pedro and my apartment in Casa de la Seda; with hindsight I should have moved out there and then, but I flew to England on 9th September 2001.

Much occurred while I was in England and time slipped away like sieved sand. Two days after I arrived back something shocking happened in America, which is now remembered as 9/11. It is firmly etched on the world consciousness, and it will be for decades to come. The eyes of the world looked on in shock as the horrific events unfolded before our eyes. Nobody could believe what they were seeing on the television or reading in the newspapers; for days afterwards, the news was saturated with pictures and reports of this tragic event. I lost count of how many times they showed the planes flying into the Twin Towers. The constant bombardment of terrifying news causes such depression and negativity so in the end I switched the television off and stopped reading the newspapers. Sending healing light to those who had tragically lost their lives and to the families of the unfortunate victims was all I could do. I also prayed for the misguided people who had perpetrated this despicable act as it is my firm belief that sending terrorist hatred only feeds the hatred that already exists.

Arthur, a dear friend of mine passed away while I was on the plane to the UK, and I was completely unaware. I realised his cancer was getting worse the last time I spoke to his wife on the telephone from La Gomera. In fact, when I was in England last April, I met them both for lunch and I knew when I gave him a hug and said goodbye it was for the last time. Feeling choked when I walked away from Arthur knowing I would never see him again was awful.

I usually know when someone close is about to cross over to the other side, but I had such a lot on my mind, and he was so concerned about his wife and family that he wouldn't have been around me anyway. Three days later I was still ignorant of Arthur's passing and with all the terrible news coming from America and worries about my house it was no surprise. I was unsettled in my sleep that night and just as I was about to dose off, I heard three loud bangs coming from the inside of the wardrobe. I sat bolt upright and straightaway I knew someone was there; it soon became clear it was Arthur. I obviously hadn't been listening in the last few days, so he had to attract my attention and he certainly did that. I asked Arthur if he could knock again another three times so I would know it was definitely him and he did. He wanted me to know he had passed away and he also gave me a message to give to his wife and kids. Of course, I was upset but I was so glad his suffering had ended. Finally, I drifted into a deep sleep with the feeling he was watching over me.

In the morning I thought how clever Arthur was to contact me in that way knocking on the inside of the wardrobe door. Of course, there wasn't a physical person hiding in the wardrobe, but I was always told to eliminate the obvious by my teacher and mentor, Gordon Higginson. Arthur always sat in my trance and physical circle and helped me organise workshops, classes, and many other events when I was working in our home-town, so it was no surprise to me. Some of you reading this book will question it happened at all, but I have no doubt in my mind.

His funeral was beautiful and moving and did Arthur justice but even though I knew he was not suffering anymore in his new surroundings I still cried all the way through the service. He was such a kind, caring and spiritual person and helped so many people in his life. After his funeral service we all went outside, and each of us let go of a purple balloon; I know he was there to watch such a lovely heart-warming spectacle.

Something else happened while I was in England. I realised there was someone else in Manuel's life. It was not too difficult to ascertain when I telephoned him from England and a female voice answered his mobile phone before it went dead. I had been in England for nearly three months as I wanted to have Christmas with the kids. He had obviously got fed up with waiting for me to return to La Gomera. I was extremely upset at first, but I had enough going on in my life and it was his loss.

Soon after Christmas I spoke to friends on the phone who told me that Lara and Ivan had been looking for me. They had decided to leave La Gomera and wanted to say goodbye. It's not easy to stay in touch with them as they hardly ever check their emails, and they don't want mobile phones and who can blame them for that; I can't imagine Lara camping out under the stars with a mobile phone ringing in her ear.

At least they were heading for Wales to visit Ivan's family so we would speak on the phone soon then they'd be off to some far off exotic place. I knew in my heart wherever they went in the world I would not lose touch with them for long; maybe for a few months at a time, but what's a few months between special friends. Anyway, Ivan's borrowed one of my precious Harry Potter books.

Christmas came and went, and my house was still nowhere near completion. Frantic calls from Annabelle, who was staying in my apartment in Valle Gran Rey, were worrying. Pedro was going crazy and told her to leave and he was accusing me of not paying the rent, which of course was untrue; Susan had given him my rent money personally. Annabelle was in a state because Pedro had sent a horrible Englishman to threaten her. He badgered her for rent money she didn't owe for the apartment she had already left; he then threw her out of my apartment. I told her not to give him any money, but she was scared. This man sounded nasty, so I booked a flight and flew back to La Gomera at the beginning of the January; not a good start to 2002.

Ignoring my feelings about Pedro in September was to prove disastrous. I had a lot of things going on in England and by the time I returned to Casa de la Seda I had no home as the so called English friend of Pedro's had moved into my apartment. My neighbour Paulette told him to stay away from her as she didn't like him at all and she's a feisty lady.

David my Dutch friend and Ramon, who is one of the few locals who speaks some English, have come with me to get my things. However, Pedro's friend is trying to persuade me to tell them to leave, so he can get me on my own and threaten me no doubt. I'm not having any of it. Arguing with the man who is doing Pedro's dirty work is draining and I don't want the lads to become embroiled. I refuse to pay rent I don't owe and demand to see Pedro but of course he is nowhere in sight. He's probably upstairs sitting in a pall of smoke from a huge joint, becoming mellow and losing a few more brain cells at the same time.

My two friends look uneasy when I stand up to this man, but they won't interfere unless they have to. None of us believe in violence and they are two very gentle men. I ask him to write me a receipt for rent paid in case there is any more trouble and after much deliberation he writes on a piece of paper. I have never felt so threatened by anyone and his aura is dark and menacing; in fact, the whole place feels sinister now he has taken it over. This man is used to getting his own way but eventually he says I can take my things; David is not letting me out of his sight while I pack boxes and bags.

Ramon, Sadie's ex-boyfriend, has a truck waiting on the side of the road. His father says I can rent one of his apartments down at La Playa. Thank goodness I'm not on my own. They load my assortment of boxes and bags onto the truck, but sadly I have many things missing; including most of the Indian jewellery I was going to sell in the market, cashmere shawls and scarves, tablecloths, napkins, cookery books and various other things. I'm upset about the portable CD player my children bought me which is nowhere to be seen. Pedro and his charming English friend obviously raided my apartment before I arrived back from England. I can't prove anything though and as the truck pulls away, I give way to tears.

My new apartment is great, and the rent is the same as I was paying Pedro, but it has much better furniture and is beautifully finished. It has a lovely bathroom and although it only has one bedroom it is large with two single beds. It also has a lift and huge roof terraces with fantastic views on all sides, including the Atlantic Ocean, valley views and down below I can see the shops and restaurants. Living further up the valley was great but it will make a change to be nearer to the beach and I'm just glad to be away from Pedro and his horrible friend.

We have finished bringing up my things from the truck and are now sitting on the terrace. Ramon can't help but see the disappointed look on my face when I notice I have no view, so I change the subject. It seems ungrateful but I know I will miss the stunning vistas I had at Casa de la Seda.

Smiling I give them a hug, "Gracias mi amigos, mucho gracias," and I hand them some local Dorrados beer. Ramon says he will take me to the Guardia Civil the next day because apparently Pedro has stolen things from Sadie too. I think too many spliffs are definitely having an effect on his brain.

David and Ramon only leave when they know I'm feeling better, and I must admit it is quiet without them. I empty a few boxes and I decide to leave the rest until the morning as suddenly I feel drained. I'm in need of a bit of peace and calm after all the awful happenings of the past few days.

Chapter Twenty-One

Intentions are the seeds
that grow into our realities,
seeds of intent are nurtured
by the water of life
and the sunshine of the soul,
be careful what you plant
in the garden of your mind.

Today I'm feeling a bit down. I've been fine for the last couple of weeks and I'm sure it's just an off day. I'm sitting on my balcony musing when I hear someone calling up to me and it's a familiar voice coming from below. Marilyn, my Dutch friend, appears like an angel out of nowhere and I lean over to wave and to let her know I'm home. She's been travelling for a few months and has just come from Southern Ireland; it's great to see her again. Marilyn lives on a small inheritance which allows her the freedom to travel, and she's decided to come back to La Gomera for a long stay. Once you've been to La Gomera it is rare you don't return. Marilyn is a spiritual lady, and this island is a spiritual place but living in Valle Gran Rey means you have to distinguish the spirituality from the claptrap.

La Gomera is often referred to as 'Hippie Island' and as I said earlier in my book it's extremely 'new age' in Valle Gran Rey; 'new age' not being my chosen words but that of the holiday brochures. There are many people here who think they are superior to others just because they've spent time in India. Or they have been meditating and practising yoga for several years. This kind of snobbery shows how little they have progressed spiritually but equally I've got to know some beautiful people.

Last week I met a truly delightful family visiting from London. They told me they were so fed up with trying to find a home a few years ago. Appalled to see so many empty houses in the borough of Hackney, in London, they started to squat. The authorities seeing how they had improved the house and how clean it was eventually allowed them to stay and rent it. He is a musician with dreadlocks and him and his wife both dress like hippies. We had a fabulous evening at La Playa when he played the guitar and sang Bob Marley, Bob Dillon, and Beatles songs; a few drummers joined in, and David was on his didgeridoo. I had to get up and dance and it was a great spontaneous party. His wife, an equally genuine person, is a midwife and they have two beautiful children. A daughter aged four and a son aged seven. Both are home educated, and you certainly notice the difference. Not having a television at home means the children have a lot of other things to talk about. They are intelligent and so polite and it's uplifting to see. Their dad stays home and looks after them while he studies Anthropology and his wife works in the local hospital on the maternity wards. They both teach their children and what a wonderful job they're doing.

They wanted to see more of the valley, so I took them to the top of Valle Gran Rey. We caught a bus up and walked all the way down which was enough for the children. It was lovely to see them interested in the environment and it became a bit of a nature trail. It is a beautiful walk from the top of the valley which I've described before; halfway there is a particularly good and popular restaurant with a terrace affording you fabulous views while you eat. The few times I've been to this particular restaurant I've had Sopa de Berros (watercress soup) a favourite on La Gomera and delicious with fresh bread; or you can have Potaje (hot vegetable soup or stew) served in traditional wooden bowls and ladles with chunks of bread. We all ate a hearty lunch and continued on our way. The children did well but dad was a bit worn out on the second stretch and he was amazed at my energy. What a charming family and although I may never see them again, I won't forget them.

It was about this time I met a twenty-eight year old young man from Germany at a birthday party. The party was for Bjourn a builder who was constructing a house in El Guro. He invited his workers some friends and a few locals and we had a barbecue in the half constructed house. It was a chilly night so there was an open fire. Dan, the young German, came to sit next to me and we got chatting. He was an apprentice carpenter in a traditional German style black suit and waistcoat, and I half expected him to start singing songs from the Student Prince. He carries a diary round with him which is stamped every time he finishes a job; there is also a code of ethics printed in the back. They are not supposed to take payment for their work, only board and lodging, but some people insist on paying them something. His carpentry takes him far and wide, and he says he loves travelling and meeting people especially as it's a far cry from his childhood spent in East Germany.

At the age of fifteen he was learning to fly a glider and he was told by 'The Party' if he flew too near the Berlin Wall he would be shot down. Most of us would find this difficult to imagine but I can't help noticing what a happy and confident young man he is. Despite bad memories of his childhood in East Germany he has a genuine smile and a hearty laugh.

German Carpenters (Dan is on the left)

He was a little over fifteen when the Berlin Wall came down and his family were listening to it all happening on the radio. It was an exceptionally emotional period and one can only try and imagine what the atmosphere was like. He says it was a shock to many East Germans, who weren't prepared for the changes to come. Suddenly they were faced with materialism and mass media, and it was hard for many of them to handle. They knew West Germany didn't really want them and it caused a lot of bad feeling. He said with conviction that many young Germans lost their way because they didn't know what the future held for them. It was a big change for the whole nation, and much healing had to be done. What an interesting and wise young man.

Tonight, I've been invited to a full moon party near Playa Inglis. As I walk down towards the beaches, I realise there isn't much of a full moon to be seen in amongst the clouds which kind of defeats the object. However, I said I'd meet a couple of musicians and I do love hearing them play. By the time I arrive and walk around an enormous circle of people only a few are compos mentis; the rest are stoned out of their heads! Various hookahs and other contraptions are being passed round and I'm beginning to feel a bit heady.

It doesn't take me long to find my two friends as they're the only two playing guitars and singing. They welcome me and a few minutes later we're having a little party all on our own. We seem to be the only ones still standing or sitting upright should I say.

The next hour is great as we sing our hearts out but I decide not to stay too long just in case the Guardia Civil have been tipped off. I don't smoke hashish whether in a hookah or rolled into a joint and I have never been tempted to try anything else either; I saw too many lives ruined when I was young. I'm not judging those who do but if there is a raid, I will be judged just by being here.

A few weeks ago, the Guardia Civil raided Playa de las Arenas (Pig Beach) and it turned nasty so I'm reliably informed. Some of the hippies and back packers make a living from crafting and selling drums. I've watched and admired their handiwork and it takes a lot of time, strength, and effort. All their drums at various stages of development were smashed to pieces by the Guardia Civil. This is not a usual occurrence and I hope it doesn't become one.

It didn't take me long to cheer up and shake off the bad feelings from Pedro and his sidekick. I went to see Paulette and she said the Englishman had gone back to England and my apartment was free again. Apparently, the flat looks an awful mess and certainly not how I left it; I didn't want to see it. What I did do though was get my computer back as Pedro had it hidden in his apartment and asked me to pay two month's rent, or he would keep it. Of course, I wasn't going to do anything of the sort because I didn't owe him any rent. Pedro's brother-in-law is a decent man and is ashamed of Pedro's behaviour; most of the locals are upset by it. He told me to demand my computer back and he would be in Paulette's apartment if I needed any help.

My lovely German friend who owns the internet café at La Playa has kindly lent me her Gomera fiancé who is a really nice guy. He's waiting by the roadside with his car so he can take me and my computer back to my new apartment. Pedro has been hiding on the roof since his brother-in-law approached him about me. Eventually he comes down after I call up to him a couple of times. Fortunately, he speaks and understands English, and it is easier to express myself in my own language.

"Pedro, I want my computer back."

"You pay me the money you owe me, and you can have it," he said as he climbed down the ladder.

"I don't owe you any money and you know it. My friend gave you my rent when she was here, and I gave last month's rent to your *charming* friend."

"You owe me money," he said as he walked to his apartment.

"You are a liar!"

He opens his front door and is about to shut it in my face when I quickly put my foot in the door and barge in.

"Get out of my apartment!"

"Not until you give me my computer." I can see it in a box, so I walk through the kitchen into the main room.

"Get out!"

"No, I won't get out. I want my computer."

"You can't have it."

"Okay, I'll call your brother-in-law shall I Pedro?" And I started to walk back towards the front door.

"Here take it," he called after me, "I don't want it anyway," and he is even carries it up the steps to my

194

friend's car; bullies are cowards and they invariably back down when you stand up to them. Even so it wasn't a very nice situation to be in.

Marilyn has met a half German half Italian guy and they seem to suit each other; he is great on the drums of which I can't resist having a go. All of a sudden, my friends, who all left La Gomera for various reasons, have returned; they all converge on me at the same time. Three of my friends are from Holland but one of them is Greek, and of course David, who still lives here, joins us. Susan is here with her new daughter, who was born in December 2001, nine months after their precious son passed away and what a beautiful baby she is. My friend Vicky is here for a two week visit and of course, known to us all, Ramon and his uncle.

We had a wonderful meal a few days ago at the Malaysian restaurant, El Baifo, owned by a lovely man who has lived here with his family for fourteen years; he absolutely adores the island. He is a wonderful chef, and the food is exquisite. The meat melts in your mouth with all the delicate flavours of Malaysia and the local vegetables are delicious and cooked to perfection. You can see he loves cooking with the way he lovingly presents each dish. We had a great time, laughed a lot, and took photos to treasure in years to come.

La Gomera is mainly a meat eating island, so El Baifo is a great restaurant to take my vegetarian and vegan friends. I like to introduce them to good restaurants especially as I can't always afford to join them. Eating out is much cheaper here than in the UK but when you live here you can't possibly eat out every night when you have visitors; besides I like to cook for myself most of the time.

We've been going to Ken's bar much more since I've been living a few doors away; it's so good to speak English and he is good company. Obviously, most of the time I speak Spanish and at least I can have a decent conversation with the locals now. The night before last was brilliant in Ken's bar but I became slightly inebriated. Did I say slightly? Actually, I was as drunk as the proverbial skunk though why the skunk was drunk in the first place I do not know. We were sitting at the bar all night with friends, and I remember singing before it all went rather hazy. Vicky had to half carry me home which luckily wasn't far and at least there's a lift. Yesterday morning I found my jeans by the front door and various other articles of clothing scattered around the apartment and my jewellery was in the bath. This morning I went into Ken's bar to apologise but he laughs and says there was no need to say sorry as we'd all had a great night.

It is Carnival once more and it will be good fun with all my friends together again. We're sitting on the beach waiting for it all to begin. Marilyn's boyfriend is playing his drums with the others while a beautiful blood red sun seemingly slips into the ocean and beams pink rays of light onto the sky. My Greek friend is dressed up as a lady of the night, but I think he might have to pay them although he looks quite convincing apart from his awful eye make-up. It's a bit worrying how much the men in Valle Gran Rey like to dress as women. Many of them look brilliant and a few have wonderful legs and its hilarious watching some of their antics; I think I'm going to be laughing and dancing all night.

The procession is fairly small compared to San Sebastian, but the floats are good and plenty of dancers and bands go by. A few men are actually dressed as men; I said a few. Some are dressed as gangsters, and they have their gangster's molls with them. After the procession the traditional dancing, singing, and chanting begins. Old and young coming together their faces the picture of joy as they keep up with centuries of tradition, followed by a fantastic fiesta. Nevertheless, by two-thirty in the morning most of my friends have gone to bed but I dance until about five o'clock.

Carnival week on La Gomera ends with a mock funeral of a giant colourful fish and is called Sardina. Again, there are a lot of men dressed up as women and many of the locals follow the fish, which is on wheels, wailing and crying. This particular tradition is enjoyed by many of the local children. It's a safe haven for them and there is no need to worry if you see them running around enjoying late night celebrations. The giant fish is pushed around the streets followed by the funeral procession until it returns to La Playa. Children walk and play alongside this pageant and take a lot of pleasure in watching the antics of the adults. At the end, the Sardina comes to rest on the beach and is set alight with fireworks inside. There are loud explosions, and the funeral procession watches it going up in flames; each time there's a spark or a bang the wailing gets louder. It's entertaining and so comical to watch.

Now carnival week is over and most of my friends have gone home I'm working in the market with what little jewellery I have left to sell. It's an early start and takes an hour to get across the island to San Sebastian but we have to leave early as it shuts about two in the afternoon. There's lots of local produce sold here and many colourful vegetables and exotic fruits are laid out on the ground in boxes, so you help yourself. I love to watch the local women examine everything closely before they even think about buying it. Wheels of creamy coloured goat's cheese with the whiff of sweaty feet are in abundance but delicious if you are partial to strong tasting cheese. Huge bright orange squashes with yellow seeds are sliced to the size you want. Everywhere home-made wines, different coloured salsas, my favourite mojo, and the delectable and sinful palm honey. The gorgeous smell of freshly baked bread and cakes wafts under my nose and bags of honey coloured biscuits are a familiar sight.

An English lady, who has lived on La Gomera for twenty-two years, sells clothes, jewellery, sarongs, cards, shawls, and scarves. She goes on long summer visits to Bali stays with friends and buys all her goods there. A German gentleman who carves things out of local wood and is extremely talented shares a large stall with his Gomera wife; she makes jewellery and various other articles. A friend of mine, who has lived here for a few years, also makes her own crafts; there is a bag stall and one selling hand painted T-shirts. The odd guitarist and violinist are playing, and a few hippies sit on the ground selling their wares. Men in their later years sit under the enormous and beautiful Indian Laurel trees. Sometimes they're called Jardin de Laurel and they give out so much energy. They also make a stunning canopy over the market square and are a wélcome relief from the sun. Elderly men and some women chat away to whoever will stop and pass the time of day with them, and many do stop and talk. Numerous people are sitting inside, and outside cafés and elderly residents sit in front of their nursing home which is next to the Columbus Museum; watching the changing scene in the market while a nun cleans the windows. The place is buzzing, and I'll be buzzing if I can make a profit today.

Chapter Twenty-Two

Secluded hamlet – Ambrosia,
hidden, deep within luscious mountains,
hitch-hikers ride to paradise.

Road ends – dirt track lures me, lined
with plants. Colours from an artist palette,
flora springing from cracks in dry rocks.

Steep climb leaves me breathless,
as do the stunning vistas. Scenery
wrapping around me like a warm embrace.

Stopping, I become bewitched, by
a valley of incredible beauty, fertile
terraces rising to the top, a giant's staircase.

No noise apart from nature's sounds,
somewhere a trickling stream, twittering birds,
humming bees searching for the drink of gods.

Nestled above me now – Ambrosia.
my spirit soars to Elysian Fields,
losing sense of time and space, just being.

Picturesque houses joined by winding paths,
entwined by multi-coloured flowers,
shimmering in the mid-day heat.

If there is a heaven on earth
then without a doubt this must be it.
Ambrosia, a hamlet as sweet as nectar.

My friends Cathy and Helen are visiting La Gomera
again but this time with another friend, Pamela, who I
haven't met before. Pamela is already enamoured with
the island. Cathy is staying with me, and Helen and
Pamela are sharing a beautiful apartment with a large

terrace looking across the ocean at La Playa. El Hierro is visible from their apartment as well and they are in the perfect spot to see the beautiful sunsets. I don't think they're particular about joining the regular band of hippies on the beach at this time of day. Anyway, they can see it all happen from the sun beds on their terrace and with a bottle of wine in the ice bucket too.

Beach life is central to many people's lives here and it's great to see crowds of eager folk waiting for the drumming to begin in the balmy evenings. For those who love percussion a treat is in store because there are a variety of drums and other small instruments expertly played. Some will even attempt to dance to the rhythmic sounds, but most are content to sit and listen. Fire eating and fire dancing is another delight, and one particular hippie makes frequent visits from Tenerife and puts on a wonderful show for everyone. He has long dreadlocks, a couple of teeth missing and wears bright, colourful clothes. He might put some people off but when you get to know him you couldn't meet a kinder or gentler man. There is also a sweet young German lady who walks up and down La Playa selling slices of apple cake and other delicious bites. She has a gorgeous baby on her hip and sells the cakes to make a bit of extra money for them. It's a great idea as sometimes you do feel peckish after having a swim and you don't always take food to the beach with you.

Playa Inglis is a nudist beach at the far end of Valle Gran Rey and the opposite end to the harbour. I have been there a few times and its undulating terrain, sand dunes, and natural environment are interesting, and it makes a change. The dunes also shelter you from the winds and I like the feeling of solitude when they separate you from the rest of the bathers. Needless to say,

I do not strip off but lie in the sun in my swimming costume. I'm certainly not a prude but I don't see the point in stripping off unless you want an all over tan which I'm not bothered about.

There is a volleyball court on Playa Inglis and it's popular with the naturists, but I cannot help chuckling to myself when watching them play; I have to stop myself laughing out loud. It's an energetic game and whilst they are running around everything is swinging about; ouch it makes my boobs feel sore. My friends Helen and Cathy would certainly give this area a miss.

Helen doesn't want to do so much walking on this visit, thank goodness, and it's not such a strain trying to please the three of them. We are having a lot of meals out and catching up on all the gossip. This time round I know the best restaurants and where to take two vegetarians and a vegan. I don't mind where we go as long as I can have a plate of freshly caught fish, preferably with the tail and head missing as I don't like the eyes looking at me, a pork chop or piece of succulent steak.

Today we are on a beautiful walk which started at Los Creces and is not too far up in the mountains. It has only taken an hour to walk through the pretty woods and I wish it had lasted longer. We have come to a delightful hamlet called Las Hayas. Helen the map reader, because no one else wants to do it, is telling us we have to go down into a deep ravine and across a rugged path to El Cercado; this where the potteries are. It's a beautiful ravine but rugged at times and hard on the calves as you scramble down the slopes on the goat's track. Finally, we arrive at El Cercado, one of the '1000 metre villages', and we take Pamela to the potteries. I have previously mentioned the potters and their ancient craft, and this is by no means the only craft on the island.

201

Weaving is prolific and extremely colourful; the rugs and covers are made in a frame from pieces of rolled fabric. Others are spun on a wheel from ewe's wool and the covers they make are exceptionally warm. I have bought myself a small, colourful rug, which I'm sure will last me for many years to come. Basket making is mainly done by the men and made from cane or sheets of palm leaves; the baskets are mostly for everyday use. Wood and leather craft is a tradition, and the goatskins have various uses, including making the skins for the traditional drums. Making the large drums is hard work and a lot of time effort and love goes into them.

We walk on to Chipude three hours after we first started out. We sit on the roadside waiting for the gua gua (bus) and watch a perfect sunset with marvellous views from this elevated village. It's an interesting area to live but they have more low cloud and not so much sun as we do down below.

The next day I decide to take Helen, Cathy, and Pamela to the 'red earth', as we call it. It's a sacred place, that's if I can find it in the car as it's well hidden from tourists; I have to remember the landmarks. Peace and harmony reign here and it's the main reason for coming to this little known part of the island near Vallerhomoso.

After driving up and down a few times I find the entrance and park easily. With relief we pour out of the hot car and start to walk along the half hidden and uneven dirt track; there are many different cacti and flora lining the narrow path. It both astounds and pleases me, that so few people know of the existence of this area. Climbing higher, but being careful not to slip on the stones, enables us to see the stunning coastline down below.

We are getting nearer to the 'red earth', actually it's terracotta, and this secluded place beckons me with its vibrant energy and absolute silence. Rain has made the earth look more orange and the ferns are a brighter green than usual; two wonderful healing colours. Wizened old trees some of which remind me of a scene from Lord of the Rings are dotted about the landscape and my favourite one looks like an old man with a beard. One part of the mountain is grey and resembles the Luna landscape with circles carved into the ground from previous earthquakes. Breath-taking views on either side are to be seen and the sea below is sapphire and turquoise.

Mount Teide looks like a pyramid suspended in mid-air as the bottom half of the mountain is clothed in a thick blue and white skirt of cloud. It's amazing up here and as Pamela has found a comfortable spot away from us to do some yoga and Cathy goes for a wander, Helen and I decide to have a meditation. The energy is positively pulsating in this unique area, and it doesn't take us long to link in. As I begin to relax and feel at one with my surroundings my meditation is interrupted when I start to sense someone close by.

"Gel, there's someone here," says Helen.

"Yes, I know I can feel him myself."

"He wants me to draw him, but I can't as I've left my pad and pastels back at your apartment."

"Oh Helen, I can't believe it, you're a Psychic Artist and you didn't bring your drawing things with you?"

"I didn't think!"

We both lapsed into silence for a couple of minutes.

"He's still here and keeps saying he wants me to draw him."

"Well ask him how you're supposed to do that with no materials."

"He says I have a piece of paper that I can use but I'm sure I haven't," she says as she starts to rummage through her bag; a few seconds later she holds up a till receipt.

"Ah this is getting interesting; you can use the blank side to draw on."

"With what?"

"Well, if he's that insistent ask *him* what you're supposed to use. He's already found you some paper, such as it is."

The energy is growing stronger, and I can see him clearer now. Helen is getting excited as this man, who looks like a hermit, starts speaking to her again.

"He's telling me he doesn't want to be drawn with manufactured pencils but with pieces of rock from the mountain so it's natural."

"Well, you'd better do as he says then!"

Helen is finding and picking up very small bits of terracotta and he urges her on to find brown and yellow pieces of rock too. Now she's sitting down and has started drawing his portrait oblivious to anything else going on around her which is how it should be. I can see his face light up as he comes close once more; he has a beautiful smile and laughter lines, deep brown eyes, and a long beard. He shows me a shack where he used to live on the side of this mountain about four hundred years ago. It was a lonely existence but one that he chose for himself. He says he is the keeper of the mountain and that is why very few tourists find this outstanding place. Helen leans over to show me the picture.

"Wow, that's brilliant."

"He says he wants me to fill the background in with some green and that I need to pick a tiny cactus leaf, break a piece off, and use it to paint."

Helen doesn't need telling twice this time and soon she's back and doing exactly what he has asked her to do. She has found a small black lead pencil in her bag and just can't resist putting the finishing touches to her portrait.

"He said he didn't want to be drawn with manufactured pencils."

"I know Gel, but I wanted to finish it off properly."

"It's great the way it is and how wonderful you've drawn him with rocks and plants just as he asked."

Pamela and Cathy have come back to see what we're doing.

If you look closely at the bottom of the picture, and behind his beard, you can just about see the writing on the back of the till receipt; unfortunately, you can't see the lovely oranges, browns, yellows, and greens that were used.

Pamela is staying with me for three more days as Helen and Cathy have now returned to England and it isn't worth her keeping their apartment on. I have driven Helen and Cathy to the ferry and now I'm driving Pamela to a few places she hasn't seen. She's a vegetarian and I know just the place to take her for lunch, Bar Montana at La Hayas. It's run by an elderly lady, Dona Efigenias. She rarely serves meat on a weekday, but they do serve meat on a Saturday when there is plenty of it and everyone sits on long tables in a relaxed atmosphere.

Canarian cooking is hearty and absolutely delicious; it's home-made cooking from what the earth produces. Cheaper cuts of meat are stewed, boiled, steamed or grilled to make tasty wholesome meals with a combination of spices, beans, vegetables and of course 'papas arrugadas'. On La Gomera the food is placed in the centre of the table, and it is acceptable to eat with your fingers. People help themselves while drinking wine, talking, laughing, and soaking up the sauces with freshly baked bread. It's a far cry from my childhood mealtimes. We were not allowed to speak, put our elbows on the table or criticise mum's cooking.

Today we are on the spacious terrace of Bar Montana, and we have eaten a lovely fresh salad with avocados. Now we have Gofio, ground and toasted maize mixed with vegetables, which you put on your plate with a large dollop of spicy mojo on the top. If tourists do not know how to eat the gofio and vegetable mixture with the mojo, Dona Efigenias, a wonderful lady, goes round to each table showing them with a big smile on her face. A filling home-made vegetable soup follows with enormous chunks of vegetables including the delicious canary potatoes, served with fresh bread and the exquisite mojo, so full of chillies and garlic. After an interval when you think you are about to burst and couldn't possibly eat anything else she brings up the home-made cake. It's the soft variety made with palm honey and is delicious. We barely have room for our gin and tonics as we sit back more than satisfied with the wonderful meal; plus, the excellent service and the beautiful view of Las Hayas from the terrace. Pamela is enjoying her last three days.

On the beach at sunset, you meet all sorts of people. A couple of nights ago I met Terry, a musician, who I recognised from last week's St. Patrick's Day gig which was brilliant, and he sang some funny songs. I wasn't expecting to be invited to a Saint Patrick's Day party in Valle Gran Rey where most people are Gomeras, and Germans and it was a pleasant surprise.

Terry lives in a wooden house right at the top of a hamlet in the mountains called Ambrosia. A hippie community have lived in these few houses for a long time, and they mix well with the locals. One of them is a schoolteacher who teaches her own and the other children in the hamlet. Terry has invited me to Ambrosia. I have wanted to go there for some time, but it didn't seem right just to turn up without an invitation.

Recently I've had the feeling that I'm going to be moving on to another island but at the moment I don't know which island or in what part of the world. La Gomera has not felt the same since my unfortunate experience with Pedro and his English friend. It's a fabulous island and the Gomeras are friendly and hospitable; many have befriended me and helped me learn Spanish, the local ways, and the history of the island. Pedro is an exception and apparently is not popular in Valle Gran Rey. However, I think it's time to move on. I said I wanted to be a nomad for a few years when I first set out on my journey, and I have to go where the spirit moves me.

I've hitched a ride halfway to Vallerhomoso and while I'm waiting at the side of the road for another lift it starts to rain but it is refreshing and doesn't last long; my pashmina has dried out already. My second lift is taking me right into Vallerhomoso where I'm going to stop for a drink and a rest. I need to mentally prepare myself for a steady climb. Not knowing whether I will get a lift to Ambrosia is not going to put me off as I'm sure it will be a beautiful walk. I will galvanize myself into action.

Walking on the tarmac road leading to my destination is pleasant but a local woman has stopped to ask me if I need a lift. She's only taking me to the lake where apparently the track to Ambrosia starts. She's not going off the beaten track herself but I'm extremely grateful to her for taking me part of the way.

It's hot and I'm lost! It seems I've walked too far round the lake instead of past it and up a steep rough road, so I retrace my steps. I meet a man with his donkey who stops to chat. He tells me to take a rest and sit on a rock with him as he points out the way to Ambrosia. Apparently, he often chats to Terry when he's up that way. However, he's becoming a bit too familiar, so I say "adios" and walk back to the point where the kind lady dropped me off earlier.

Here the roadway turns into a dirt track which thankfully has been flattened recently. It's so steep it's taking my breath away. Remarkable scenery is also taking my breath away and it's worth every step to see the thick, luscious valley and the colourful plants. Spring flowers are on either side of the pathway and are growing between the cracks in the rocks. Stopping several times,

I listen to the birds singing and witness once again the beauty of nature until I spy the pretty hamlet resting in a niche above me.

It's still a long walk through the hamlet to Terry's house which is at the uppermost point of this valley, but I receive a warm welcome when I finally arrive. There are four of us for dinner; a young lady who is going to look after Terry's house and garden while he's away in Ireland and an Arabic man who lives in the hamlet with his wife and children. A vegetable dish and mixed salad, all grown in Terry's garden, are going down well with mixed rice. We sit on cushions on the floor and eat off a low table which I'm now used to doing.

His beautiful wooden house nestles right at the top of this huge canyon and is enclosed by a succulent, thick green covering; it's no wonder he has a fertile garden. He grows lots of fruit and vegetables and even a few banana trees interspersed with flaming red Geraniums.

The house itself is sturdy enough with a small kitchen and a large main room with guitars hanging on the wall and a drum kit in the corner. A few chairs, the low table and coloured cushions are scattered around. The main bedroom is upstairs on a mezzanine; to get to the spare bedroom, where I'm sleeping tonight, you have to go out of the house and round the back. This is where the bathroom used to be, and I don't know why Terry got rid of it; he doesn't seem to mind doing his ablutions outside in the garden, but I find it quite an experience. I've had to get out of the habit of drinking from cups and saucers but to do without a bathroom is another matter altogether. It's okay for one night but I've decided I'm going to leave first thing in the morning. Also, I want to see the sunrise over this magnificent and secluded part of the island and to be able to enjoy the walk down before it gets too hot and sticky.

Having said my goodbyes the night before, I rise just before daylight. My futon was comfortable enough, but the bedding looks like it could do with a wash. I'm sure there were a few insects sharing my room; nothing seemed to trouble me except a scratching noise during the night. Some creature wanting to share my room. Needless to say, I did not open the door and invite it in.

Walking round to the back of the house I search for the moon which is still hanging over this sleepy hamlet and the sky is brimming with stars. At least the moon is lighting my way as I creep across the garden to the earth closet; I don't want to wake Terry. In case you've never used such an enclosure the only way is to straddle the dugout crouching as we ladies do; ignoring the deposits below which haven't been covered over from the night before. I hope there are no peering eyes amongst the trees. Not that I'm too bothered about someone catching a glimpse, but they might think the moon has dropped out of the sky.

Back in my little room and relieved in more ways than one I tidy up the bed. Putting a few things in my rucksack and grabbing my precious notepad and pen, I smile to myself after my encounter with the earth closet. That's not bad for someone who eighteen months ago would not even consider going behind a bush.

Day is just beginning to break over this stunning part of mother earth and there is complete silence as I start my steep descent. A bit further on the birds are beginning to chirp intermittently bringing a smile to my face. Soon the whole valley is bursting forth in one grand chorus of song; a dawn chorus the like of which I have never heard before. Every blade of grass, every tree, every bush, the sky above and the earth beneath me seem to be a part of this wonderful symphony and I feel at one with all that is. I wish I had thought to put a recorder in my rucksack but instead I will have to remember this amazing sound and enjoy the moment.

There is a line of palm trees are at the end of the garden, thick plants, bushes, and I can hear a stream running underneath which I hadn't noticed yesterday. A wonderful fragrance is filling the air and I'm reluctant to leave this sweet-smelling spot, so I stay still for a few minutes enjoying the moment. A bit further down the track there are two colossal aloe vera plants on my left and for a few seconds I think John Wyndham's 'Triffids' have returned yet again.

There are white and grey clouds rolling over the peaks of the mountains and a couple of fluffy peach clouds in the otherwise clear blue sky; the sun rises over this cloistered hamlet. Looking down onto the pretty red tiled roofs as I walk down the winding steps and through Ambrosia, I marvel at the houses enveloped by nasturtiums and marigolds; it's like walking through an English country garden. It's a mistake to say all hippies are dirty and messy because this protected hamlet is extremely well looked after. The children have a wonderful education and start in life the like of which couldn't be imagined by most families living in inner cities.

Further down there is a larger hamlet slumbering quietly. Land is so fertile here and looking across the valley you can see hundreds of farmed terraces. It's a flourishing farming community and I can't believe how high some of the terraces go. The sides of the gorge look like a giant's staircase and from where I'm standing it looks impossible to get to the highest ridges. Fortunately, they still have the Astia on La Gomera a kind of pole vault about two metres long. It's usually made from beech wood, covered with a soft charnal, and has a metal point at the end. The farmers hop at great speed flying along precipices with the ease of acrobats thereby shortening the distances they have to cover.

Another tradition is 'silbo' the whistling language which has survived for many centuries by being passed down from father to son. It has enabled the men to communicate with each other over long distances and it still echoes in the interior of the island. It is an authentic language and even has different accents and tones according to which part of the island you come from. This whistling language penetrates valleys and huge cliffs and even through mountainous areas; it was, and still is, the most natural form of communication despite modern methods.

White clouds now take on a pink hue as golden sunlight flows into this huge canyon. It looks greener than ever after the heavy downpour last night; like a gigantic green, billowing rug. Looking back, I can just about see Terry's wooden house at the top of the valley and the hamlet is sitting sheltered above me. Below are palm trees, bamboo, gorse bushes, aloe vera, numerous fruit trees and in between the terraces are dry stone walls. Only the melodic sound of birdsong breaks the silence but as if to stop me floating off into the clouds there is the sudden unexpected noise of a car behind me. I recognise the occupants from Ambrosia and the driver offers me a lift. I decline his offer because I don't want to miss anything in this place of outstanding beauty as I meander along the dirt track lined with spring flowers.

Each time I go round a bend in the track the scenery changes. I'm nearing the bottom of the gorge but if I sweep my eyes round to the left there are many undulating hills hugging tiny hamlets. Round another bend and in front of me is the huge freshwater lake and it's like someone changing slides on a projector. Once more I want to freeze the frame but know I cannot and it's another reminder to live in the present.

On this beautiful lake which is a nature reserve there are ducks, swans and it is full of fish; spectacular purple flowers are growing along this side of the lake. Looking over my shoulder towards the gorge I have just walked down all I can see now is a mass of bamboo. I'm nearing the end of the dirt track as I slowly walk round and admire the lake. It's good to be on the tarmac road once again and there are so many colourful bougainvillea clad houses of all shapes and sizes; some backing onto this beautiful expanse of water. I could not live in an isolated hamlet like Ambrosia but here I can't think of a more appealing place to make one's home; however, I find myself saying that on a quite few parts of this glorious island.

Sun slips behind El Hierro, floating
like a pancake in The Atlantic Ocean;
tiny paradise on earth,
undiscovered by the masses.
Wispy white clouds,
like an old crone's hair combed through,
disintegrate in minutes,
as vapour from a kettle.
Orb of liquid light,
edged with luminous pink
is sucked into the sea;
twilight beckons – a new island,
another adventure.

Soon I will return to England for my 50th birthday party and it will be a good time to consider a new milieu and another adventure; it feels like a time of completion on La Gomera. Ambrosia is an exquisite hamlet and a credit to the hippies who live there. If there is a heaven on earth, then this must be it. It's a remarkable part of the island to visit before moving on to pastures new. Following the celebrations my children have planned I will return to Valle Gran Rey, pack up my things and say my goodbyes. By then I'll know where my new abode will be and one thing, I do know for sure it will be on an island; island life suits me, and I love to be surrounded by the ocean.

My mother still makes it clear she doesn't approve of my new life; it used to upset me enormously, but I don't allow it to anymore. I am who I am, and I follow my destiny. I'm happy in my own skin and although this took me many years to achieve it was worth it. My son makes jokes about my bohemian lifestyle and my stock answer to this is, 'Do I care?' It's not good to let people's judgements stop you being yourself. My children love me the way I am even though they'd prefer me to live in England.

It's goodbye to La Gomera. I'm thankful and I hope a little wiser for the lessons I've learned. I have treasured memories of the island and of the many interesting people I've met. Special friends are valuable, and I've made a few on this magical island some of whom have already moved on themselves. By the time I leave I will have been here for twenty-one months and what an eventful twenty-one months it will have been. On La Gomera there are so many delights, so many stunning views and so many surprises. There will always be a little piece of my heart on this wonderful Island.

On this stunning island,
where settlements and farms
occasionally fuse into hamlets,
the king of birds – the hoopoe,
with crested head, rests in trees
on the rustling palm fronds;
subtle wind music murmurs
in your head, as the breeze
runs its fingers through the lush valleys.

Island of cliffs whipped by winds,
weather-beaten in sun and rain;
luminescent colours,
run through layers of prehistoric rock,
yielding ancient vertebrae.
Valleys where the night sky is so clear
the sliver of new moon dazzles;
an aged star, like a bejewelled earring,
hangs on its cusp.

An unspoilt island, La Gomera,
where the moon waxes and wanes
with delirious abandonment,
and the poet is free
to drift without a compass;
faraway from life in the city,
where her soul would weep tears;
when the island recedes,
the king of birds still nests in palm trees.

The End

Printed in Great Britain
by Amazon

81424678R00122